# Criminal Justice Research in Libraries

# Criminal Justice Research in Libraries

## Strategies and Resources

Marilyn Lutzker and Eleanor Ferrall

Foreword by Edward Sagarin

GP GREENWOOD PRESS
NEW YORK • WESTPORT, CONNECTICUT • LONDON

**Library of Congress Cataloging-in-Publication Data**

Lutzker, Marilyn.
Criminal justice research in libraries.

Includes indexes.
1. Reference books—Criminal justice, Administration of. 2. Criminal justice, Administration of—Bibliography. 3. Library orientation. I. Ferrall, Eleanor. II. Title.
Z5703.4.C73L87 1986 364'.0722 85-17765
[HV7419]
ISBN 0-313-24490-1 (lib. bdg. : alk. paper)



Library of Congress Catalog Card Number: 85-17765
ISBN: 0-313-24490-1

First published in 1986

Greenwood Press, 88 Post Road West, Westport, CT 06881
An imprint of Greenwood Publishing Group, Inc.

Printed in the United States of America

The paper used in this book complies with the Permanent Paper Standard issued by the National Information Standards Organization (Z39.48-1984).

10 9 8 7 6 5 4 3 2

# Contents

# List of Charts

# Preface

As librarians and teachers who have spent many years sharing library usage techniques with students and other researchers, we recognize their need for a printed resource guide for criminal justice research. The idea developed of merging input from a librarian in a midsize specialized college in a large eastern metropolis with input from a librarian accustomed to a large university in the West. We feel the book has benefited greatly from this merger of small and large, specialized and general, East and West. To compile such a resource sounded—and proved to be—challenging.

Not the least of the challenges was to gear the material to the reader. And we knew full well that the reader might be a full-time practitioner with theoretical or technical needs, a student either new to college or new to criminal justice studies, a professor seeking ideas for student research, or an independent researcher. To be all things to all persons proves impossible. Therefore we offer theoretical overviews, tried techniques, basic information, and clues to further sources. We encourage you to utilize those sections most applicable to your own unique needs.

Few authors ever achieve alone; we are no exception. We are grateful to Edward Sagarin, author, researcher, scholar and gracious gentleman, for his erudite introduction. We extend sincere appreciation to Eileen Rowland, chief librarian of the John Jay College of Criminal Justice, who spent hours with us in discussion, read all or substantial parts of the manuscript during its several stages, and offered many valuable ideas. We thank Dr. Donald R. Riggs, director of University Libraries, and Carolyn Dusenbury, head of Reference Service, both of Arizona State University, for their unerring support throughout the project.

Valuable criticism and help were forthcoming from Anne Larsen, Antony E. Simpson, and Bonnie R. Nelson, all of the John Jay College of Criminal Justice, and Carol Ruppe, Rosalinda DeFato, Julie Olson, and Nancy Manning of Arizona State University. The interest, support, and patience, during our "distraction," of the staffs of both libraries were remarkable. We are grateful. From our students over the years, we learned much. Our editors Mary Sive, Dolores M. B. Abbott, and Cynthia Harris offered help along the way.

Finally we thank our families. Some couldn't really escape the highs and lows; they exhibited welcome and deeply appreciated forbearance and encouragement. Others, being far afield, contributed in other ways.

We add the traditional caveat: we assume responsibility for all errors of commission or omission.

M. L., New York City
E. F., Tempe, Arizona

# Foreword

*Edward Sagarin, City University of New York*

Crime is often said to be as old as time, or at least as old as life. These are metaphorical statements, for what is meant is that crime is as old as *Homo sapiens*. No other species, form, or variety of living organism has the wisdom to make laws nor the urge, motivation, and ability to violate them.

To paraphrase a famous sentence in sociology, written not about crime but about social inequality, crime is traced back to antiquity and extends to ubiquity. Although criminal behavior had been noted for centuries in the first criminal codes and by literary artists and philosophers such as Sophocles and Aristotle, the first serious inquiry into the nature of law-breaking and what ought to be done with those responsible for harm to others did not occur until the eighteenth century.

The great literary event that marks the birth of the literature on crime came in 1764, when Cesare Beccaria, a young Italian nobleman with no experience or previous knowledge in the field, wrote his treatise on crimes and punishments. His theories were based on the premises that governmental policy should seek the greatest good for the greatest number of people, that surety of punishment, not severity, effected security and order, and that the severity of punishment should be scaled to the severity of the crime. He taught that anything in excess of these principles led to tyranny. Beccaria's small book attracted attention and had an influence throughout Europe that must have taken its author by surprise. It was almost immediately translated into English, French, and numerous other languages. It seriously influenced the thought of such diverse and important thinkers as Voltaire in France and John Stuart Mill in England, and it led to legislative reform of criminal justice practices in western Europe, England, Russia,

Sweden, and eventually America. The followers of Beccaria's theories became known as the *classical school* of criminology, its first and founding school.

In revised form, Beccaria's influence was most undeniably felt in the early years of the nineteenth century when the Napoleonic Code was promulgated. That Code, reflecting the influence of Beccaria but with modifications which allowed for some mitigation and flexibility, became the basis for the criminal code in most continental European and Latin American countries. The revisions in Beccaria's theories, however, were sufficient to give this development a slightly different name; it was to be called the *neoclassical school*. In some instances it showed a remarkable similarity to what was to appear a century and a half later under the concepts of just deserts and retribution.

To trace what has happened in the literature of crime, and eventually what came to be known as criminal justice, in the almost two centuries since the Napoleonic Code, would be a formidable task requiring several volumes. Here only a few highlights will be mentioned and a few landmarks cited; many will be omitted, deliberately or inadvertently.

The early and middle years of the nineteenth century brought two developments of great importance to the social sciences and to criminology. The first was the study of social events in a systematic, scientific manner, following the rigorous methodology of the physical sciences. The most important single name associated with this work was probably Auguste Comte, who coined the term "sociology" and conceived of the study of social phenomena as something that would be in the nature of what was called "social physics." His influence was wide; the setting was established for the birth of what is today termed the social sciences.

The second event of equal or perhaps greater importance in the eyes of many was the publication in 1859 of *The Origin of Species* by Charles Darwin, initiating what some have called "the century of Darwin." For Darwinians, biology was paramount, and all aspects of the world could be thought of in terms of evolution and survival of the fittest.

Directly related to these two events was the emergence of what has been called the social survey or social reform movement. Born in response to the extreme social problems of the nineteenth century, this was a movement not of scholars but of philanthropists, journalists, and other individuals who united for social action. They felt that amassing all the facts about the human social condition would lead to solutions for such problems as poverty, health, education, housing, crime, and prison discipline. The writings of these people were not intended as scholarly and scientific works, but were social statements aimed at informing and molding public opinion and influencing social policy.

The synthesis of the two great philosophical forces represented by Comte and Darwin was manifested by the emergence, in the latter quarter of the nineteenth century, of Cesare Lombroso. An Italian physician who worked with criminals, particularly in the army, he founded with many of his contemporaries what came to be known as the *positivist school* of criminology. Its controversial nature notwithstanding, it soon gained prominence and, temporarily at least, left the classical and neoclassical schools as nothing more than moments in history. Lombroso's name is often associated, particularly by people who have only the most superficial knowledge of his work, with born criminals, atavistic evolutionary throwbacks, and physiological signs (or stigmata) by which such persons could be recognized as criminals. In the totality of his work, however, and particularly in its later stages, he thought of many of these criminals as having developed because of social conditions and others as having inborn criminal tendencies or predilections that made them vulnerable to crime under certain conditions. This position was remarkably similar to that taken in the latter part of the twentieth century by researchers promulgating what is now called the biosocial basis of violent behavior.

Thus, with Beccaria's social philosophy and Lombroso's statistical studies and systematic investigations, there came into existence criminology, and later, in a distinction that is still not entirely clear, criminal justice.

On the European continent, criminology and criminal justice developed as subdivisions of criminal law and were dominated by people learned in the law and occasionally in psychology. In England and the United States, a separate course of development took place. Criminology came to be taught almost entirely within sociology departments, but it was taught as a concentration on crime, delinquency, and, a little later, deviant behavior, within the larger field of sociology.

Neither of the two approaches proved adequate for two reasons. The first is that crime, with its form and shape, its frequency, its perpetrators, and the nature of the reaction against it, has to be studied in an interdisciplinary fashion. This means that theories and writings from the disciplines of political science, economics, psychology, anthropology, philosophy, and criminal law, to name a few among many, must be integrated with one another.

A second reason that criminology or criminal justice could not be adequately served as a subdiscipline of either sociology or criminal law was the growth of a separate, independent literature seldom studied by those trained either in criminal law or in sociology, although it was not entirely ignored by either. That literature specialized in police science and administration on the one hand, and punishment, imprisonment, rehabilitation, and what came to be called so optimistically and euphemistically "corrections," on the other.

This brings us to a few more highlights which are necessary to describe how we got to where we are. Throughout the nineteenth century, theories of imprisonment and punishment attracted great attention in the United

States. What came to be known as corrections had its associations, conferences, and position papers in America considerably before sociology, criminal justice or criminology had gained any academic or scholarly recognition.

Not until the later years of the nineteenth century, with the dominating figure of William Graham Sumner at Yale University did American universities first grant recognition to sociology. In 1893, the University of Chicago offered what is believed to be the first doctorate in sociology, and two years later it initiated publication of the *American Journal of Sociology*, which continues to be published. In 1905 a group of sociologists met and formed the American Sociological Society, which several years later initiated publication of its own journal, *American Sociological Review*, which also continues to be published.

The focus of attention and the center of study in sociology during the first quarter of this century was undoubtedly the University of Chicago, where what came to be known as the Chicago school of sociology was taught and practiced. It is difficult to pinpoint exactly what constituted this school, other than its excellence, the large numbers of outstanding people who graduated from it, and the dominant position that it held. The Chicago school urged its students, faculty, and researchers to go out among the people, live with them, and see how they lived in order to study the real world of real men and women. In addition to a focus on crime, deviant people, and lower socioeconomic classes, the Chicago school developed the idea of the "own story" or "life story" of individual criminals, often carefully annotated by a criminologist, a lasting contribution to the burgeoning discipline.

Also in Chicago, but at Northwestern University School of Law, an American Institute of Criminal Law and Criminology was formed, growing out of a national conference. Soon after, the School of Law launched its excellent journal—the only law school journal in which criminal law was not just paramount but exclusive: the *Journal of Criminal Law, Criminology, and Police Science*. It was an interesting title, for it represented a marriage that many did not believe the scholars and the disciplines were ready to put into effect. Police science was later dropped from the title; perhaps it suggested too much the practitioner for a scholarly journal. The journal is today known as the *Journal of Criminal Law and Criminology*.

Many other events of the twentieth century can be quickly recorded. Two organizations in the fields of criminology and criminal justice were formed in addition to the many established in corrections, police, and related areas. Each assumed importance, held national conferences, distributed newsletters, published journals, and established networks of people who came to know each other's work and often to collaborate. The American Society of Criminology started issuing a journal called *Crimi-*

*nologica*, a title later changed to *Criminology: An Interdisciplinary Journal*. The American Society of Criminology attracted mainly academic people, primarily from sociology but not to the exclusion of professors of criminal law, psychiatry, and other disciplines. Then the Academy of Criminal Justice Sciences (ACJS) was formed, with a greater practitioner emphasis, but nonetheless scholarly, and with some overlap in membership between the two organizations. The ACJS holds an annual conference and publishes *Justice Quarterly*. Yet these are only two of the many journals—regional and specialized, some having ideological views—that now fill the shelves, or at least the microfilm drawers, of a good library in this area of study.

Academicians, practitioners, and students became increasingly interested in the distinction, if any, between criminal justice and criminology, particularly as the former term began to be used with greater frequency. The development of a field of scholarly studies, based around the practitioner aspects of those involved in the prevention, control, and management of crime and the handling of those found guilty of criminal acts, appeared to many to be both possible and important.

A forerunner in this field in America was August Vollmer. On the West Coast he started a police training program in 1908. Five years later this became the Berkeley Police School. Today, Vollmer's association with the first major effort to bring professionalism to police and scholarship to the study of problems in policing is symbolized by an annual award, named after him, given each year by the American Society of Criminology to an outstanding practitioner. Later, the University of California at Berkeley formed a School of Criminology, as distinct from a school of social sciences or a department of criminology. It taught both the academic and scholarly aspects of criminology, with a sociological emphasis, but it also had a training program in forensic sciences. The political turmoil of the late 1960's led to the disbanding of the school, though not before it had launched some major publications on crime from a radical or Marxist perspective.

To return to the distinction between criminal justice and criminology, some scholars would contend that the names are interchangeable, but others, myself included, disagree. Both have as their focus the understanding of crime, the event, and the perpetrator. Criminology places this in the context of society, power, legislation, and causality and sees crime primarily in terms of the universality of social norms and the causes of and reaction to their abrogation. Criminal justice concerns itself with crime and its societal context but puts equal emphasis on police science and administration, on criminal law and the court system, and on jails, prisons, and alternative forms of punishment.

In 1965 there were 95 academic criminal justice programs in the United States of which only 9 included graduate-level education. Ten years later there were 1,348 such programs, including 185 at the graduate level. The establishment of the Law Enforcement Education Program (LEEP) as part of the Law Enforcement Assistance Administration (LEAA) had had a major effect.

With the increase in criminal justice programs as a result of LEEP and other forces, with the expansion of research as a result of grants from the LEAA and numerous other government and private agencies, and with the tremendous attention given to crime by the public as a result of the great increase in crime and violence from the early 1960's through the 1970's, the amount of information available to the criminal justice researcher started to multiply. As in many other fields, there was an information explosion. At first there were but a few journals printing articles on crime; then came the deluge. There were not only journals specializing in criminal justice but hundreds of others in related fields that included articles on crime. Abstract services were devoted to crime, police, and other fields of study, but articles on crime were also abstracted and indexed in publications devoted to psychology, sociology, and medicine, among others. And then there were the innumerable government documents; the material found as chapters in books (books not edited by the chapter authors and hence not cataloged under their names), in newspapers and in magazines; and countless indexes. There were dictionaries, encyclopedias, histories, biographies, and volume upon volume, row upon row of opinions from numerous courts. All this is in print, in computer files, on microfilm and microfiche.

This veritable deluge of data, statistics, information, ideas, texts, and documents is so overwhelming that one wonders how a young profession could ever have advanced without it. It is also so overwhelming that one is intimidated and does not know where to start or how to get at that small portion of what is there that is essential to one's own needs and interests. The scholar gets lost in a maze because the information is so extensive and so rich. But such information has value only to those who can locate it. That is where the expert, not in criminology but in librarianship, becomes essential. This leads us to this excellent book, so needed that we can only look to the void that it has filled and ask ourselves, in disbelief, how we ever functioned before. The answer is simple: many of us did not know that the gap existed.

Now the drudgery of finding information can be simplified and reduced in time—time better spent on reading, thinking, testing, writing, and going forward from the point where one has stopped learning what others have done. To make this possible, Marilyn Lutzker and Eleanor Ferrall have done a superb job. Our indebtedness to them will be apparent from the first page. I hope for the sake of research and scholarship that our colleagues in other disciplines are as fortunate in finding people equally knowledgeable and devoted to write guides for library research in their fields that deserve to be on the same shelf with this book.

# Part 1

# BEFORE YOU START

# I

# Introduction

The purpose of this book is to make the process of library research logical, efficient, and—hopefully—interesting for its readers. Professor Sagarin's foreword offers an impressionistic history of the origins and growth of the field of criminal justice studies. The chapters that follow should help students and researchers find their way through the labyrinth of documentary material related to those studies.

When a research area is relatively new, most participants know the projects on which their colleagues are working. The scholar can keep up with new ideas in the field through an informal network or through membership in one or two appropriate organizations. But as the number of researchers and specialties within the field grows, reliance upon personal contacts becomes hazardous as a way of keeping up with current research. A more formal, organized method of locating information becomes essential. The need arises for a bridge that will connect the reports of individual primary research—the substantive literature—and the person looking for that information.

Fortunately for researchers in criminal justice, as in most other academic fields, these bridges—in the form of research tools—seem to develop as the fields themselves develop and expand. The information exists; the need for the information exists; the research tools evolve in response to that need. Chart A is a schematic presentation of this process. It shows selected highlights in the historic development of criminal justice studies, which were discussed in the Foreword, and some key bibliographic responses to that development.

It is rare for a beginning researcher not to feel overwhelmed by the size of the task, the number of decisions to be made, and the seeming impos-

## CHART A.

### SOME HIGHLIGHTS IN THE DEVELOPMENT OF CRIMINAL JUSTICE AND SOME OF THE MAJOR RESEARCH TOOLS WHICH SERVE IT

#### SOCIAL SCIENCE AND SOCIOLOGY

**1876**-First American Sociology course at Yale University

**1893**-First Ph.D. in Sociology offered at University of Chicago

**1895**-*American Journal of Sociology*

**1905**-American Sociological Association

- 1907-*International Index*
- 1928-32-*Social Science Abstracts*
- 1930-*Encyclopedia of The Social Sciences*
- 1953-*Sociological Abstracts*
- 1968-*International Encyclopedia of The Social Sciences*

#### CRIMINOLOGY

**1899**-Lombroso's *The Criminal Man*

**1923**-First B.A. with minor in Criminology

**1941**-American Society of Criminologists

- 1961-*Criminology and Penology Abstracts*

#### CRIMINAL JUSTICE

**1916**-Vollmer's Police School

- 1929-Kuhlman's *Guide to Material on Crime and Criminal Justice* (first comprehensive book-length bibliography)

**1963**-Academy of Criminal Justice Sciences

- 1975-*Criminal Justice Periodical Index*
- 1981-*Encyclopedia of Crime and Justice*

#### POLICE AND LAW ENFORCEMENT

**1845**-New York City establishes first professional police force in America

**1893**-International Association of Chiefs of Police

**1909**-U.S. Bureau of Investigation (later called F.B.I.)

- 1931-*Uniform Crime Reports*

**1968**-Law Enforcement Assistance Administration

- 1973-*Police Science Abstracts*

#### PENOLOGY and SOCIAL REFORM

**1764** -Beccaria's *Essay on Crimes and Punishment*

**1790's**-Beginning of experiments in penal reform in New York and Pennsylvania

**1845**- *Journal of Prison Discipline and Philanthropy*

**1865**- American Social Science Association

**1870**- American Correctional Association

- 1897-*Encyclopedia of Social Reform*

sibility of knowing not only what should be the first step but what should be the second or the third step. The library building itself can be intimidating: large, seemingly unorganized, and filled with an overwhelming quantity and variety of materials. Even experienced researchers—indeed, even experienced librarians—often feel disoriented and confused in an unfamiliar library. Be assured that the more you use the library, and the more you know about it and its resources (including the librarians), the more comfortable you will feel.

One way to achieve that comfortable feeling is to use this book in the manner in which it is designed: read this introductory chapter, chapter II, and perhaps chapter III, *before* turning to other parts of the book. They will help you to vault the preliminary hurdles.

Chapter II, "Communication, Information, and Information Flow" provides a generalized overview of how information is generated and communicated by criminal justice researchers and practitioners. Each of the forms in which information may be transmitted is discussed and related to the type of library tool that can provide access to that information. This is the chapter which will give you the theoretical basis for deciding where to start your research. It may well be the most important chapter in the book.

Chapter III, "Efficiency in Research," is designed basically for the neophyte researcher, although even the more experienced might find it helpful. It deals with some of the mechanics of getting started and organized and contains advice aimed at conserving both time and temper.

Chapter IV, "Bibliographic Searching: Computer and Manual," describes the most modern method of locating information sources and puts it in perspective in relation to traditional methods.

Part 2 assumes that both mood and method are under control. It discusses the different kinds of available resources chapter-by-chapter and offers nitty-gritty details about how and when to use specific items.

Part 3 expands on three special kinds of research situations: legal research, historical research, and comparative research.

The appendices, as appendices always try to do, contain generally useful information which did not fit conveniently into any other place.

# II

# Communication, Information, and Information Flow

## COMMUNICATION

Professors have plagued students for generations with a famous philosophical problem: if a tree is felled by lightning in a totally deserted forest with no living thing to hear it fall, did it make a noise when falling? How can we know?

### Formal Communication

Communication of research results may be compared to the tree falling in the empty forest. One may call research results data, information, knowledge, or facts; whatever the label, if they remain known to only one person, there has been no communication. If there is no communication, is there any value to the research?

Publication of research results has traditionally been the formal method of communication. Public, formal information sources are available to those who know how to gain access to them. Restricted, formal information sources are available only to those entitled to access them. Whether public or restricted, these sources are in permanent form and are independent of any one individual. This published communication of research results, with its subsequent validation, analysis, and synthesis, constitutes the literature of a field.

This literature, the formal communication system, can be viewed as a continuum. It moves from the substantive information, both professional and scholarly, at one end, to the bibliographic records or citations which identify that information at the other.

### Informal Communication

Communication may be informal as well as formal. The informal communication network is basically one person talking or writing directly to someone else. Although no attempt may be made to keep the information secret, its existence is not publicly known. Hence, it is unavailable to anyone outside the network of colleagues or friends. When these informal networks are strong they can be very effective.

## INFORMATION

Communication transmits information in many ways and in many formats. Awareness of the distinctions between primary and secondary information sources and among scholarly, popular, and professional literature is essential for the researcher.

### Information Sources: Primary and Secondary

To the scholar, and to the student, the distinction between primary and secondary sources can be vital, even though to the world in general it often seems to matter little.

#### *Primary Sources*

Primary sources are raw data or information without analysis or interpretation. They are the building blocks from which the analytical literature of the discipline is built.

The form of a primary source may differ from one discipline to another. Failure to understand this is one reason for confusion about the meaning of the term. For the historian, a primary source can be a document written on vellum or an ideograph carved in stone. For a political scientist a primary source can be a printout of voter records; for a sociologist, a returned survey form. For a scholar in criminal justice it could be any of the above or a report of the results of an experiment in dispute resolution by police officers.

As a source of information upon which to base conclusions, a primary source, to the scholar, is always preferable to a secondary one. Primary sources vary in their reliability, or authority. Criteria generally used in evaluating the degree of authority of a primary source are: (1) the closer to the activity documented, the better it is as a record of that activity; the immediate testimony of an eye witness is probably more reliable than recollections written fifty years later; (2) the less selectivity involved in documenting the event, the more reliable is that documentation. Thus, a verbatim transcript of a trial or a press conference is more authoritative than the newspaper story reporting the event. It is not uncommon for the same document to contain primary data of different degrees of authority and also secondary analysis.

Even the most popular communication forms—newspapers and television—can be sources of primary data, but great care must be exercised in evaluating them. The television film may show the event, but someone exercised discretion in deciding where to point the camera; the journalist had to decide which parts of the story to emphasize and whom to interview. These problems are discussed further in chapter VI.

### *Secondary Sources*

Secondary sources involve the selection, evaluation, analysis, or synthesis of data or information. They may be based on a single primary source or may draw upon multiple sources, both primary and secondary.

Secondary sources most often take the form of articles and books. However, the distinction is in the substance of the material and not in its format. It is possible for a report to be mainly evaluative and analytical and thus secondary in nature and for the book format to be used for presentation of primary material.

The same source can be both primary and secondary depending upon how and when it is used. The 1897 *Encyclopedia of Social Reform* is today a primary source for anyone interested in tracing the history of concepts and movements in social reform, although it was basically a secondary source when published. Today's newspaper editorial describing mismanagement in the prison system is a secondary source for the researcher interested in prison administration but might be a primary source for one interested in attitudes toward prisons and prison administrators. In fifty years it could be a primary source for one interested in either topic.

## Information Sources: Popular, Scholarly, and Professional

The distinctions between popular, scholarly, and professional literature are important for the researcher to recognize. However, one must keep in mind that the differences are not necessarily in the substance or quality of the information but rather in its presentation, which is determined by the intended audience.

### *Popular Literature*

Popular literature is that written for the average adult information seeker who wants facts or opinions presented clearly and succinctly. Detailed descriptions of methodologies employed would be both unnecessary and unwelcome. The reader does not intend to replicate the research process but relies on the author to have used reliable sources and to have covered the topic thoroughly. If the reader disagrees with the conclusions in the article, he or she will drop the article and attempt to find a more congenial author. Popular literature is often well researched, even though not always according to strict scientific procedures. Examples of popular sources are newspapers and magazines such as *Time* and *Psychology Today*.

***Scholarly Literature***

Scholarly literature is that written by and for an audience which needs to know not only the conclusions but the manner in which they were drawn. The reader is interested in methodology and precise identification of sources. Good scholarly articles are written so that the reader learns the derivation of every piece of information and every idea not original to the author. The text can be used to retrace the research and check it with the original sources if there is any doubt as to the validity of the conclusions. Examples of sources in which such articles appear are *Criminology: An Interdisciplinary Journal*, a commercially produced journal from Sage Publications, and *Justice Quarterly*, an official publication of the Academy of Criminal Justice Sciences.

***Professional Literature***

A category which sets criminal justice apart from the more traditional academic disciplines, professional literature addresses the day-to-day problems of practitioners as distinct from the concerns of academics. As practitioners (although they may be scholars as well), these readers have policy and action as their main considerations. The position of the person who did the study may be of more interest than its research design and methodology. They are less likely to seek evaluation of the design of a study than identifiable and positive results directly applicable to their own problems. Examples of these types of articles may be found in journals such as *Corrections Today*, the official publication of the American Correctional Association, and *Police Chief*, published by the International Association of Chiefs of Police.

## INFORMATION FLOW

Knowledge starts with an idea, an observation, a concept, a theory in need of testing or elaboration. An overview of new ideas or theories as they move from inception to acceptance and inclusion within textbooks and encyclopedic tomes shows a generally similar progression through several identifiable stages. This movement is called the information flow.

The stages in this flow of information follow a basic pattern, although there are uncounted possibilities for variations due to the complexities of both research studies and researchers. The following hypothetical case is offered as an example of the movement of information within the criminal justice system.

The director of a large halfway house for juveniles believes that a certain type of educational program will reduce recidivism among juvenile offenders. The idea is discussed with staff, friends, and colleagues, and a research study is designed to test the hypothesis. Applications are made for research funding from the institution itself, a government agency, or a private foundation. When the funding is received and work is ready to begin, the project will be announced to criminal justice colleagues in the corrections or juvenile justice newsletters and to the broader community through local newspapers.

While the project is underway, the director may again bring it to the attention of the criminal justice community by presenting a paper at a professional conference. When the study is finally completed a report of the findings will be written, submitted to the funding agency, and circulated within the criminal justice community. The information in the report is now public.

If the findings appear to be significant, someone within the agency, or perhaps someone from the wider criminal justice community, may write a journal article discussing them. The article, or the original report, may inspire other researchers to attempt replication of either all or part of the original study, perhaps expanding it to encompass additional related hypotheses. Additional reports and articles will in turn generate further discussion. As the ideas achieve wider circulation they will be reported and discussed in books. Eventually, if widely accepted, they may appear in summary form in textbooks and encyclopedia articles.

In the above hypothetical example, it is possible to isolate seven distinct points in the flow of information: (1) informal discussion; (2) announcement in newspapers and newsletters; (3) conference papers; (4) formal reports; (5) journal articles; (6) books; and (7) textbooks and encyclopedias. At each of these points the communication occurs in a different format. Since most library research tools are designed to locate information in only one or two formats, access to the information flow varies. The information flow, and its access points, is illustrated schematically in Chart B.

Although the subject matter at these seven steps could remain the same, at each level of communication there might be a meaningful shift or change in interpretation or conclusion. This could happen as the original idea is expanded or contracted, unexpected subtleties arise and are dealt with, and methodologies are refined.

### Discussion with Friends and Colleagues

This is the informal communication network. It provides the most up-to-date information. Unfortunately, it is available only to those within the network of friends and colleagues. Informal networks exist in both the agency and academic worlds and in their interstices.

**CHART B.**
**INFORMATION FLOW, AND ACCESS TO INFORMATION, IN CRIMINAL JUSTICE**

| FORM OF INFORMATION | TO LOCATE THE INFORMATION, USE: | FOR DISCUSSION SEE CHAPTER |
|---|---|---|
| WORD OF MOUTH | | II |
| NEWSLETTERS | CRIM. JUSTICE PERIODICAL INDEX | VI |
| NEWSPAPERS | NEWSPAPER INDEXES | |
| NEWS BROADCASTS | BROADCAST INDEXES | |
| CONFERENCE PAPERS | IF PUBLISHED, IN:<br>• PROCEEDINGS IN PRINT<br>• INDEX TO SSH PROCEEDINGS<br>• SOCIOLOGICAL ABSTRACTS | VII |
| REPORTS and DOCUMENTS | INDEXES TO REPORTS and DOCUMENTS | VII |
| JOURNAL ARTICLES | JOURNAL INDEXES and ABSTRACTS | VIII |
| BOOKS and MONOGRAPHS | LIBRARY CATALOGS | IX |
| SUMMARIES, OVERVIEWS, HIGHLIGHTS | •ENCYCLOPEDIAS<br>• ANNUAL REVIEWS | V |

### Announcements to Newspapers and Newsletters

When the grant is received and/or the project started, it will probably be announced and described in the publications of the granting agency, the newsletters of the criminal justice profession, and possibly in the local newspapers of the community. Although the example with which we have been working involves an agency, research grants for both empirical and theoretical studies are available to academia as well.

Information in newsletters and newspapers is part of the formal information network. It can generally be located through use of appropriate indexes and abstracts (see chapters VI and VIII for further discussion).

### Conference Papers

The ideas and possibly some interim reports on the progress of the research might be presented at a conference of scholars or criminal justice practitioners. Copies of papers presented at such conferences are made available to those who attend the conference. They may also be published in conference proceedings, and occasionally some are summarized in newsletters or newspapers.

Presentation of papers at a conference is somewhere between the informal and the formal; some information is available in printed formats, and the careful researcher can locate it, although not always easily. The section of Chapter VII on conference proceedings has a full description of the available tools.

### Reports

At the conclusion of the study, a report will be written. This report may vary in form from a full-scale book printed in large quantities and widely distributed to a short, informal document. These reports can be written by an academic, a practitioner, or a person with a foot in each camp.

The formal report of a research project is generally called a research report if it is undertaken by a private agency or individual and a government document if it emanates from a government agency.

Because of the variety in format there are many ways to locate reports and documents, ranging from the general library catalog to highly specialized indexes. It is important for the researcher to know the intricacies of locating these sources, because the information they contain is frequently unavailable in other formats. See chapter VII for a full discussion.

### Journal Articles

Journal articles are frequently the next stage in the information flow. In the example we have been using of the agency research study, someone responsible for the research might write an article for a professional journal reporting the nature of the study and its conclusions. On the other hand, an academic associated with the project, or one who learns about it and is interested in the subject, may write an article for a scholarly journal discussing the study. In both these instances the information conveyed is very likely to have appeared at one of the earlier stages of the information flow.

In the academic world, journal articles often represent the first step rather than an intermediate one in the process of information transfer. With the exception of those instances where there have been government grants, the newspaper/newsletter and report stages will not be involved. Scholarly journals are the key devices for transmission of ideas within the scholarly community.

Whether they represent the first stage or an intermediate one, journals are one of the most important sources of information for the criminal justice researcher. Articles may be located by use of the appropriate indexes and abstracts which are discussed in detail in chapter VIII.

### Books

With the research reported and communicated to the profession, the ideas can now join the body of analytical literature in book form. Some studies by academics make their first appearance in books. Efficient and effective use of the library catalog to locate books is discussed in chapter IX.

### Summaries and Overviews

As the idea circulates more widely and becomes accepted and integrated into the literature of the field, it is eventually incorporated into textbooks and encyclopedias. The research is now integrated into the knowledge base of the discipline.

## INFORMATION FLOW: THE ACADEMIC AND THE PRACTITIONER

The information flow of criminal justice might be said to move in parallel streams: the academic, the practitioner, and the overlap represented by the person involved in both worlds. It would be nice if we could firmly assert that the branches function as a team with constant interaction between them. In truth, evidence suggests that the ideal is not the actual, in this case as in so many others.

Practitioners and agency personnel, even those with academic connections and backgrounds, are concerned with the vital problems of the here and now. They may not always think in terms of preserving the records of their research or of ways to make the results available to others. Once a study has been completed and implemented, the written report no longer has any pressing value to the agency. It may be filed and forgotten. Academics and personnel from other agencies might hear about it through the informal information network, but its long-term utility to scholars and historians might be largely overlooked in the press of daily agency concerns.

On the other hand, practitioners, although they may be desirous of theoretical support for their arguments, frequently do not have readily available the access tools to locate the more formal research of their academic colleagues. Even where the tools are available, the time traditionally involved in locating relevant academic research may not appear as cost-effective to the busy administrator. There is the possibility, however, that the use of microcomputers for online bibliographic searching, full-text retrieval, and document ordering may change this in the near future. (See chapters IV, VI, and VIII.)

## INFORMATION FLOW INTO CRIMINAL JUSTICE

No profession or academic discipline functions in an enclosed bubble uninfluenced by other fields. This is particularly true of criminal justice.

A criminal justice researcher must be aware of the possibility of obtaining information from the many fields which intersect and feed directly into criminal justice. Although there are variations in the manner of information generation and dissemination in each of these fields, the basic movement of information and its relation to access tools are similar. Some interdisciplinary aspects of criminal justice research are quite obvious. It is hard to deal with problems of search and seizure without dealing with constitutional law. One cannot discuss the problems of literacy in the prison population without dealing with what the education profession has learned about adult literacy programs.

In other cases, more imagination is needed to assess possible information rewards from allied fields. For example, if you are interested in problems of police stress, the literature of psychology will tell you about the psychology of stress; the literature of public administration or business administration may discuss on-the-job stress, and the literature of sociology may discuss the dynamics of constant work in small groups (such as two people in a patrol car). If you are interested in behavior modification as a rehabilitative technique in prisons, you may want to know what psychologists say about behavior modification, but you must also know what the law says about the civil rights of prisoners. Research studies of any depth into almost any problem in police administration would benefit from information derived from the fields of public administration, business administration, communication sciences, and political sciences.

INFORMATION FLOW INTO CRIMINAL JUSTICE

See Chart C for a schematic representation of the interdisciplinary nature of criminal justice research.

## ENTERING THE INFORMATION FLOW NETWORK

The key point for the researcher to understand is the nature of the information flow and to decide where to plug in to that flow. If a commanding officer wants to know which departments in the state are currently conducting research on community relations with non-English-speaking minorities and needs the information in one day, it is best to plug into that informal network in the fastest way possible. On the other hand, if what is wanted is a thorough review of all such programs currently underway, and you have a few days leeway, it might be best to go beyond the informal and work down the information flow through newsletters, newspapers, and journal articles.

If, however, you need to get a fast overview of the problems of probation before deciding on a research topic you might want to start at the other end of the continuum with the synthesizing and summarizing literature.

Breaking into the information flow at an appropriate point is not difficult. Just as there is an overall logic to the manner in which information moves, there is also an overall logic to the tools which have been developed to enable researchers to access that information.

Reference tools have been developed which serve as connectors between the researcher and both the substantive information and the citations which lead to that information. Knowing the manner in which information flows within the field, and the appropriate reference tools for locating that information, is one key to efficient and effective library research.

# III

# Efficiency in Research

Few, indeed, are those who find valuable research material through serendipity. Only the rare researcher can rush into a library at the last moment, check a few references, digest limited information, and compile an acceptable report. For most persons library research is a time-consuming, sometimes confusing, project, followed by the challenge of writing a cohesive report. Although this chapter is directed primarily at the neophyte researcher, even the more experienced may find one or two helpful ideas.

## A MASTER PLAN

Every project will benefit from a master plan, the framework of efficient research. Step-by-step the researcher should:

1. Choose a topic;
2. Draft an outline;
3. Master the arrangements and procedures of the library to be used;
4. Consider the information flow;
5. Establish parameters;
6. Maintain a research record;
7. Build a bibliography;
8. Locate the needed materials;
9. Master a citation format;
10. Choose and use a method for taking notes;

11. Revise the outline;
12. Write the paper.

These steps tend to merge one with another and may not inevitably follow this exact sequence. As you find, read, and analyze material, you may be led to additional important citations that induce you to alter your original topic and outline. Following a master plan in general, however, will assure orderly progress toward your goal of efficient research.

## 1. CHOOSE A TOPIC

Choosing a topic is the first and sometimes the most difficult step in writing a paper. Professors may give students the freedom to select a topic, hoping that personal interest will foster finer research. The student, on the other hand, faced with such a broad choice, may be at a loss for ideas. If you are in the latter situation, help is available. You may turn to:

- Encyclopedias: the overview and organization of material in an encyclopedia may indicate topics worthy of investigation and expansion.
- Periodical Indexes and Abstracts: scan the subject indexes in recent issues for indications of topics of current concern.
- Textbooks: chapter headings and subheadings may suggest areas for research.
- Discussions: talks with professors, professionals, coworkers, librarians, and fellow students can reveal questions in need of answers and comments in need of clarification or rebuttal.
- *Library of Congress List of Subject Headings*: your library will have this list either bound or on microfiche. Selected lists of Library of Congress subject headings related to criminal justice are provided in Appendix A of this book. Scan these lists for topic ideas.
- Published lists of suggested term paper topics. You'll find such guides listed in the library catalog under the subject heading "research reports."

Be sure to choose a subject you find interesting. The topic you choose must be sufficiently limited in scope to allow for reasonable coverage in the length of your paper. It must be sufficiently broad to allow you to locate enough information about which to write. If you consider doing a comparison, be wary. Comparisons tend to double the required research. And as the old adage goes, time is of the essence. You must plan to spend enough time doing the research to capture the essence of your topic.

If actual time in the library, as well as time in general, is your problem, choose your research topic with this in mind. Although every topic requires some work in the library, the relationship between time needed for work in the library and time needed for work at home can vary considerably.

Research that centers around recent events and new ideas is likely to require the use of journals and newspapers which, even when they can be photocopied, take considerable library time, especially if they are on microfilm. A topic that relies heavily on statistical sources will require considerable time in the library, since in most libraries statistical publications are noncirculating. On the other hand, long-standing controversies and well-established concepts are likely to be well covered by books which can be read at home.

## 2. DRAFT AN OUTLINE

Your preliminary work does not have to be done in a library. Thinking is a vital part of your research process; it can be done almost anywhere. Thinking carefully about your outline in the beginning will save you time later.

If you did not use an encyclopedia to find a subject, this is a good time to consult entries relevant to your topic for general background information.

Now, write a preliminary outline. It may be very broad. It will probably list questions or concepts rather than specific facts. Keep the outline tentative and flexible. It will undoubtedly undergo several revisions.

At this stage if you do not feel comfortable preparing an outline, do more background reading. List questions you need to answer. Ask yourself, "What do I want to know?" The more you learn about the topic, the easier it should be to prepare your draft outline. If it is not, you should rethink your choice of a topic. You may choose to do only one aspect of your original topic, or you may want to select another one.

## 3. MASTER THE LIBRARY

To work efficiently in any library you must know how it is arranged. Most libraries in the United States arrange their books according to either the Dewey Decimal System or the Library of Congress Classification Schedules. Both systems bring together items on the same subject. Even libraries that use the same classification schedules may vary considerably in the arrangement of their resources. Most libraries distribute maps and floor plans to acquaint you with their facilities. Request one. Once you know where things are located you will not aimlessly roam the stacks and waste time.

In becoming acquainted with the library be sure to note where the reference librarians are located. They are the single best source of information in the library. Don't overlook them.

Learn the library's procedures. What materials circulate? What identification will you need?

## 4. CONSIDER THE INFORMATION FLOW

If you skipped, skimmed, or did not fully understand chapter II, go back and read it now. It is a vital part of organizing your research plan. Note the various forms in which information may be found. Do you really need to utilize all elements of the flow, or can you intercept the information flow at a specific point? Which type of information source is most likely to yield the material needed for your project? For a short paper a few carefully selected periodical articles may give you all the material you need. For a very long paper you may need to do a complete review of the literature, utilizing the entire range of sources. Most research projects fall somewhere in between.

Always keep in mind the interdisciplinary nature of criminal justice research. For example in considering prison industries you may have to look at the literature in the fields of business and politics, as well as corrections. In researching a topic such as the use of hypnotism in criminal investigation, you might want to read the opinions of psychologists and people concerned with civil rights law, as well as those of persons concerned with law enforcement. If you are writing on vandalism in state parks you will search public administration resources. In almost every case be prepared to use indexes from related subject areas.

## 5. ESTABLISH PARAMETERS

Armed with knowledge of the general pattern of information flow, a subject, and a draft outline, you should decide the parameters of your research before you start. Some parameters are almost mechanical. Either with your professor, or alone, you have determined the length of the paper, the currency of the material to use, and the amount of subjectivity which will be acceptable. Your outline will help establish parameters on the depth of research required.

## 6. MAINTAIN A RESEARCH RECORD

Keeping a research record may sound as though it will take extra time. Actually, it is a procedure designed for people who have little time or who must do their research in small segments of time. Consider the advantages such a record offers:

1. It is a visual record of the sources you will use;
2. It enables you to proceed in an organized fashion;
3. It keeps you from backtracking if you are interrupted;
4. It enables you to utilize effectively even very short periods of time.

In your record you should:

1. On a separate card or sheet, list each source to be searched—be it a library catalog, index, or abstract:
    a. Consult with your librarian for possible indexes and abstracts to list;
    b. Remember to include indexes to government documents and reports, if appropriate;
    c. Make separate cards or sheets for each catalog, if you are using more than one catalog or more than one library.
2. List on each card or sheet, if applicable, what issues of that source you will search:
    a. If you are confining your research to the latest five years, list only issues for those five years;
    b. Check off each issue as you finish reviewing it.
3. List on each card or sheet the subject headings or terms under which to search in that particular source:
    a. Remember there is a wide disparity of indexing terms among catalogs, indexes, and abstracts;
    b. Find out which indexes and abstracts have their own thesaurus or list of subject headings used in that index. Examine these for usable terms. If no thesaurus exists, write down possible terms. As you work with each source, add or delete terms;
    c. When you look at an actual catalog entry under the subject headings you have chosen, see if there are numbered tracings, or added entries, under which the item is also cataloged. They may be at the bottom of the entry. You may find valuable subject headings there to add to your list;
    d. Use the Library of Congress subject heading lists, or the "Selected Lists of Library of Congress Subject Headings," printed as Appendix A of this book.

## 7. BUILD A BIBLIOGRAPHY

When you find items that will be useful to you, list the full bibliographic information, either on your cards or on separate notebook sheets. It is vital that bibliographic citations be legible and complete. Most librarians can tell dozens of horror stories about frenzied late-night telephone calls begging for one piece of missing bibliographic information.

At this stage do not attempt to be too evaluative. If the item seems useful, list it. You can discard superfluous materials later. Also, do not be hampered by the suspicion that your library might not have an item. If the library does not own a title it can often be obtained from another library.

## 8. LOCATE MATERIALS

Locating materials is a largely mechanical procedure but one which frequently requires more time than the average researcher considers reasonable. Ideally, everything you need can be either checked out or photocopied. In reality, you will probably hit some snags.

If you are unable to locate things on the shelves find out if your library provides a search service for items that appear to be missing. Will the library recall titles you need if they are checked out on long-term loan? Will it accept reserves for items being used by another patron?

Acquaint yourself with services to obtain books and journals which are not in your library. Many libraries now have available, either in print, in microformat, or on computer, catalogs of other libraries to aid you in locating material. Most libraries provide an interlibrary loan service which will obtain needed material for you from other libraries; some belong to local and regional consortia which permit patrons to borrow from any member library.

## 9. MASTER A CITATION FORMAT

If you look in the subject section of a library catalog under "report writing" or "research" you will find books telling you (1) how to cite and (2) how to write.

Books which tell you how to cite materials are called *style manuals*. These began as lists of rules for printers to use in setting type. They have evolved into books of rules for writers to use in preparing papers, articles, and books. Take time to study the style manual you will use. Here, in detail, are the formats and mechanics for presentation of your research. Pay particular attention to the preparation of footnotes, or endnotes, and bibliographies. Master the kinds of information needed for each and the mechanics of its arrangement. Stick to the main formats; exceptions can be checked later. If you do not purchase a copy of the style manual, or even if you do, make a sample copy of the basic examples to keep with your research record. Such practice assures that you will record complete information in the required format.

Possible style manuals to use include:

Campbell, William G., Stephen V. Ballou, and Carole Slade. *Form and Style: Theses, Reports, Term Papers*. Boston: Houghton Mifflin, 1982.

Gibaldi, Joseph, and Walter S. Achtect. *MLA Handbook for Writers of Research Papers*. 2nd ed. New York: Modern Language Association, 1984.

*Publications Manual of the American Psychological Association*. 3rd ed. Washington, DC: American Psychological Association, 1983.

Turabian, Kate L. *A Manual for Writers of Term Papers, Theses and Dissertations*. 4th ed. Chicago: University of Chicago Press, 1973.

If no specific manual is recommended, you might find this title convenient to use:

University of Chicago Press. *The Chicago Manual of Style: For Authors, Editors and Copywriters.* 13th ed. Chicago: University of Chicago Press, 1982.

## 10. CHOOSE AND USE A METHOD FOR TAKING NOTES

For years writing guides have recommended cards for maintaining bibliographic records and for taking notes. Some guides even discuss the relative merits of the various sizes and colors of cards. It is a time-proven method. In the past decade, however, many people have forsaken the taking of notes for making photocopies, either of entire articles or of pertinent sections. Commuter students and part-time researchers in particular may need to collect materials in the library and do their reading and evaluation at another time and place.

Many people today also feel it is faster to highlight important paragraphs than to take notes and copy quotes by hand. Saving time is their major consideration. Be aware, however, that the very process of note taking involves analysis of the material which can then be incorporated directly into your paper. Use of photocopying can reduce time spent in the library, but reliance on photocopying to the total exclusion of note taking may actually make the process of synthesizing information more difficult in the end.

When researchers make extensive use of photocopying, their notes end up measuring 8½ × 11. If this is the method of research you use, then it is more efficient for you to list your bibliographic sources on separate sheets of paper that can be interfiled easily with your photocopies. Don't forget always to identify the source of your photocopy.

As you collect your notes, be sure you understand plagiarism. All direct quotations, borrowed ideas, and visual material such as tables or cartoons must be documented.

Remember that most access tools do not give you qualitative assessment of the resources you have chosen. You must analyze your information, discovering its strengths and weaknesses, comparing and contrasting ideas for variations and similarities. Research can be defined as a systematic inquiry into a subject in order to discover and revise facts and theories.

## 11. REVISE THE OUTLINE

Having gathered your material, taken notes where necessary, and evaluated the substance of your sources, go back to your draft outline to add the extra details you have learned about your topic. Often the material, as you evaluate it, falls into logical segments. Take advantage of such natural divisions. The more detailed the outline you produce at this point, the less rewriting you will have to do.

One final note: be prepared to discard some of the material you have collected. Not everything that sounded great at one point in your research will be usable now. Padded papers may look impressive, but professors and editors generally like them lean.

## 12. WRITE THE PAPER

If you haven't done much writing recently (or ever) you may want to look at some books that discuss writing techniques. Try one of these titles:

Flesch, Rudolph, and A. H. Lass, *A New Guide to Better Writing*. New York: Warner Books, 1982.

Runkel, Philip J., and Margaret Runkel. *A Guide to Usage for Writers and Students in the Social Sciences*. Totowa, NJ: Rowman & Allanheld, 1984.

Strunk, William, Jr., and E. B. White. *Elements of Style: With Index*. 3rd ed. New York: Macmillan, 1979.

Zinsser, William. *On Writing Well: An Informal Guide to Writing Nonfiction*. 2nd ed. New York: Harper & Row, 1980.

Other guides offer tips on the methodology of assembling a research paper. With variations, they will discuss the sequence of sections of a research paper, outlining, sentence structure, grammar, and punctuation, plus suggestions for making the job easier.

Flynn, James, and Joseph Glaser. *Writer's Handbook*. New York: Macmillan, 1984.

Hodges, John C., and Mary E. Whitten. *Harbrace College Handbook*. 8th ed. New York: Harcourt, Brace, Jovanovich, 1977.

# IV

# Bibliographic Searching: Computer and Manual

## BIBLIOGRAPHIC SEARCHING

"Searching," once considered a buzzword of computer technology, has been integrated into the linguistic flow of the library's jargon and the researcher's vocabulary. First used in conjunction with data bases available only online, the term now encompasses indexes, abstracts, and catalogs, whether online, in print, or in microformat. Searching means to examine a source systematically in order to extract the information you need. You will hear the word searching frequently in the course of your work. What both experienced and inexperienced researchers need to investigate is the relationship between searching by computer and searching manually. At times, one or the other may prove essential in accessing items of potential use in your research.

## COMPUTER SEARCHING

For most researchers the paperless library and the videoscreen librarian are still fantasies of the future. What today's researcher can now utilize is the online data base, an electronic warehouse of stored information. Online means that information is stored in machine-readable format and can be directly extricated by a searcher using a password, a computer terminal, a telephone connection, and the proper protocol, or commands. This procedure is called computer searching.

Computer-searching technology entered the library world in the early 1970's. Producers of specific indexes and abstracts contracted with vendors to make such products available online. The vendors, in turn, sold access to these data bases to libraries, businesses, organizations, and public agencies. Approximately 800 data bases are now publicly available from vendors such as BRS (Bibliographic Reference Service), Dialog (Dialog Information Systems, formerly a division of Lockheed), and SDC (Systems Development Corporation), using its *ORBIT* software.

### How Computer Searching Works

A computer search locates information in a machine-readable data base, just as a manual search locates information in the printed index or abstract. In most cases, the product of a computer search is a printed list of citations to articles, books, reports, or documents. The list can be either printed out immediately online or printed later (offline) by the vendor and mailed to you at home or in the library. Abstracts are available in some data bases. There are also some data bases from which a searcher can print out actual statistical data or the full text of an item, rather than citations that lead to the literature.

Librarians who offer computer search services have been trained in the protocol necessary to search a vendor's system. Each vendor establishes its own set of commands that must be used to recall information.

Data bases are indexed, and thereby searchable, in a variety of ways. Most searching is done by name, by a subject descriptor, or by keywords that appear in the title and abstract.

### Searching by Name

A citation containing a person's name can be retrieved from a data base whether the person is the author, the subject, or only mentioned in the entry.

### Searching by Descriptor

Descriptor is online jargon for what is called a subject heading in the library catalog. All items on the same subject, in the same data base, will be indexed under the same term. Many data bases have their own thesaurus, or list of descriptors, used for that specific data base. In other cases, the searcher must rely on familiarity with the data base or the researcher's knowledge of the subject to isolate relevant terms.

### Searching by Keyword

Any significant word used in a title or abstract is a keyword. In general, every data base entry is indexed not only by descriptors but by every one of its keywords. Thus, if a standard descriptor is not available or does not retrieve what is needed, the searcher can enter any word which the researcher considers significant in describing the topic. If that term appears in either a citation's title or its abstract, that citation will be retrieved. Finding citations by entering keywords is called free text searching.

### Boolean Logic

Using a concept called Boolean logic, the computer can combine subjects and coordinate concepts. Boolean logic is a procedure which employs the words "and," "or," and "not" in order to match terms. It can be used whether searching by name, descriptor, or keyword. For example, you plan to write an article comparing and contrasting jails and prisons. By using the "and" command you will retrieve those articles in the data base which discuss both jails and prisons.

AND

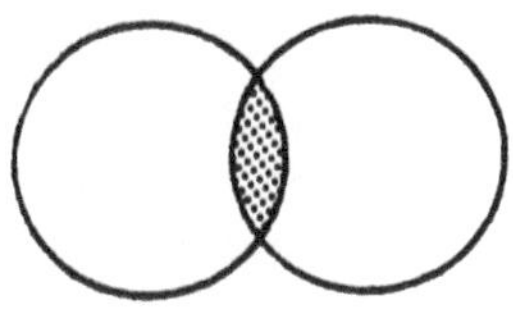

JAILS AND PRISONS

By using the "or" command, you will broaden your search and retrieve articles that discuss either jails or prisons.

OR

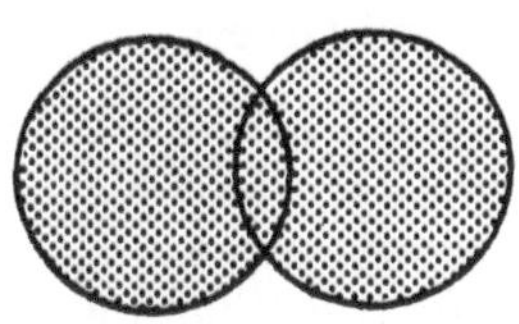

JAILS OR PRISONS

If you want to retrieve articles on jails alone, not those which also include a discussion of prisons, you can eliminate the latter by using the "not" command.

NOT

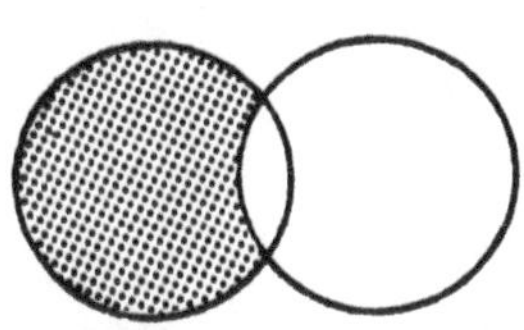

JAILS NOT PRISONS

Boolean logic controls the method of matching terms and consequently both the quantity and quality of items retrieved through computer searching.

### Having a Computer Search Done

If you are interested in a computer search, consult your librarian to discover the extent of available search services. If the service is available on your campus and if a search seems advisable, you may need to complete a form which asks for your research topic, a brief summary of the information required, and possible keywords useful in searching. Discuss with your librarian the choice of data bases to search. Criteria may include the match between your topic and the subjects covered by the data bases, the type of journals indexed, the time period, and the availability of abstracts. Usually, the librarian will set up an appointment to run the search. The librarian/searcher will need time to develop the search strategy. Remember that time spent in consultation and on planning search strategy before the actual search is time well invested. Pausing for discussion and decision making while online will increase the cost of the search.

Many searchers encourage the researcher to be present at the time the search is run. There are often choices to be made online that the researcher should make. If very few citations are available, should the search be broadened in some way? If too many are noted, should it be limited by another concept or within a time frame? The researcher knows best what is needed. If only a few citations are available and the material is needed immediately, the researcher may want the items printed online. Instant access may offset the increased cost of using computer time. Otherwise, citations can be printed offline and mailed. The expense is less, but the material will take a few days to arrive.

### Computer Searching in Agencies and Offices

With some variations the procedures described above are followed in businesses, organizations, and public agencies which provide access to online data bases. The person responsible for searching may be called an information specialist, but the methods will fall into similar patterns.

One criminal justice agency that provides remote searching is the National Criminal Justice Reference Service (NCJRS). At your request and for a fee, staff there will prepare a computer-generated bibliography with abstracts of items in their data base which match your research needs. The address for NCJRS appears in chapter VII.

### Advantages of Computer Searching

Saving time for the researcher is the most obvious advantage of computer searching. Within several minutes, for instance, the computer can scan every issue of *Dissertation Abstracts* from 1861 for works on hung juries. Done manually this would take many, many hours.

Currency of information is another advantage of searching by computer. Information loaded into a data base tends to be retrievable much earlier than that from a printed index.

Free text searching has the advantage of having current terminology or buzzwords immediately available for retrieval. Such terms appear as keywords in titles and abstracts long before they become authorized subject headings. This capacity to search by using the author's language greatly increases the number of access points to information and the number of citations retrieved.

Boolean logic allows you to combine multiple concepts in a manner not possible in manual searching. A greater measure of precision is achieved, thereby assuring that retrieved items will be on target. In addition, the capacity to enter multiple terms for the same concept insures that pertinent items will not be overlooked because of variations in terms.

The end product of a computer search is custom made for your individual research needs: a printed bibliography, specific data or information, or even the actual text of an article.

### Disadvantages of Computer Searching

Cost is one of the disadvantages of computer searching. The actual cost of a search is determined by the vendor. At present it may be based on the amount of time you are connected to the computer and may also include a set amount for each citation recovered. Computer time costs and citation charges differ greatly from one data base to another.

Methods of charging for computer searches vary widely among libraries. Some libraries charge researchers the cost as billed by the vendor; others add a surcharge to the vendors' charges; others have a flat fee for every search. Some do not charge patrons but absorb the cost into their own budgets. Many libraries, especially those that charge, will run searches on any requested topic appropriate for the data bases available. Other libraries will exercise more discretion and run only those which their personnel believe meet their parameters for online searching.

Not all disciplines are well covered by machine-readable data bases. Similarly, not all printed data bases in a discipline may be available online.

In many instances a computer search is not necessarily an exhaustive, or even a comprehensive, search of a subject. It must be considered as one source for research, not necessarily the exclusive one.

Researchers using computer searches lose the advantages of browsing and serendipity, finding valuable items by accident. These advantages should not be underestimated. With a computer search you get information only under the terms you request.

Using a computer for a short paper requiring only a few citations may be overkill. You may have to sort through more items than is necessary for the sources you need.

### End-User Searching

As the months go by computer searching will be done not only by librarians and information specialists but by the end user, any individual with access to a telephone, a microcomputer, and a modem (a device which links your computer to that of the vendor via telephone lines).

The proliferation of microcomputers in offices and private homes has motivated data base vendors to provide user-friendly, menu-driven systems at reasonable rates for use directly by such individuals. Menu-driven systems allow you to instruct the computer by choosing the next action from a menu, or list of possibilities, provided directly on the screen. Bibliographic data base pioneers in this area are *BRS After Dark* and Dialog's *Knowledge Index*. Both are available during their companies' nonpeak usage hours, utilize simplified procedures, and limit the number of data bases available for searching.

If you utilize a microcomputer to do your own searching, you have the advantage of doing the search at your own convenience, perhaps more quickly and less expensively. You may, however, face the loss of a skilled intermediary trained in the complexities of computer techniques and knowledgeable about the strengths and idiosyncrasies of available online data bases.

### Trends in Computer Searching

What we write today about computer searching may change next week. Trends certainly indicate increased usage of microcomputers in conjunction with searches, specific data bases available on laser discs and sold by subscription, proliferation of menu-driven systems, use of public telephone lines, charges billed to credit card numbers, software that translates a generic search into the protocol of multiple vendors, and increasingly more direct involvement of the end user in the searching process. Your librarian can help you keep abreast of these developments.

## MANUAL SEARCHING

Manual searching is the procedure with which most of us are familiar. It means that you physically examine each index, abstract, or catalog, looking under selected index terms, subject headings, keywords, or known authors or persons in order to locate items of potential use for your research.

### Advantages of Manual Searching

The performance of manual searching can be a learning experience in itself. It acquaints the researcher with those access tools pertinent to the literature of the field. The eye may capture related, or even unrelated, sources of information of use now or at a later date. There is a serendipity in manual searching that is achieved in no other way.

The work can be done at times that fit into the researcher's own schedule rather than that of the librarian doing the computer search. The researcher is not dependent on an intermediary's expertise and understanding of research needs.

Manual searching avoids the expense of paying computer costs in those organizations which charge for computer services.

Finally, you have access to a wider range of the bibliographic resources of criminal justice, not just those available in machine-readable format.

### Disadvantages of Manual Searching

Manual searching may require a greater investment of time than computer searching. You spend time not only looking for sources of information in an access tool but also in copying the citations.

Access points in most research tools are limited to an indexing term or subject heading, the author, and, possibly, the full title.

In addition, manual searching does not provide for the combining of concepts. If you are studying performance evaluation of correctional officers you may have to check under both terms to retrieve all the relevant information.

## MAKING A CHOICE

In choosing between computer searching and manual searching the researcher's first problem is still to define the subject; to establish its parameters; and to decide which forms of information, as described in chapter II, will best yield the quality and quantity of information needed. The next step is to determine whether such forms are more easily accessed by computer. If so, does the investment of funds offset the investment of time? Does the subject require the use of Boolean logic to match terms or concepts? Finally, should one method or the other be used exclusively, or does the topic require a combination of both?

## DATA BASES AVAILABLE

An ever-increasing number of information sources are available for online searching. Throughout this book we have noted machine-readable resources. Check especially chapters VI, VII, and VIII.

# Part 2

# LOCATING INFORMATION

# V

# Encyclopedias, Dictionaries, and Annual Reviews

Despite the existence of a general, popular conception of what should be contained in an encyclopedia or dictionary, those who compile and edit such books are a very diverse group, and the range of information contained within them is surprisingly varied. Chart D summarizes selected features within some of the encyclopedias and dictionaries discussed in this chapter.

The distinction between encyclopedias and dictionaries is fairly clear to the average person. A dictionary gives definitions; an encyclopedia has articles. Somehow this clear distinction has been somewhat muddled by publishers, leading to multivolume "dictionaries" containing long articles and single-volume "encyclopedias" containing only definitions. The distinction in the title does not matter; what is important is to know where to look for what kind of information.

## ENCYCLOPEDIAS

In chapter II we discussed encyclopedias as frequently representing the last stage in the pattern of information flow. After an idea or fact has circulated and has been accepted within the scholarly community, it finds its way into those forms of secondary literature that are designed to cumulate, synthesize, and summarize the information of the field. Foremost among these cumulating and synthesizing sources are encyclopedias.

Encyclopedias have suffered from bad press; they are frequently thought of as primarily for children, as unscholarly, inaccurate, and as unsuitable sources for the serious student or researcher. This reputation is unfortunate and usually inaccurate.

## CHART D.
### SELECTED ENCYCLOPEDIAS AND DICTIONARIES:
#### SUMMARY OF FEATURES

| | Ency. of Crime and Justice | Guide to Amer. Law | Ency. of Psychology | Scott, Concise Ency. of Crime & ... | Sifakis, Ency. of Amer. Crime | Williams, Dict. of Amer. Penology | Gaute, Murderers' Who's Who | Nash, Almanac of World Crime | Nash, Look For the Woman | Rush, Dict. of Criminal Justice | DeSola, Crime Dictionary | D'Auria, Legal Terms & Concepts |
|---|---|---|---|---|---|---|---|---|---|---|---|---|
| Biographies, extensive | 1 | ● | ● | ● | ● | ● | ● | ● | ● | | | |
| Biographies, short | 1 | ● | ● | | | | | ● | | ● | | |
| Biographies of criminals | 1 | | | ● | ● | | ● | ● | ● | | | |
| Specific Crimes | ● | | | 2 | ● | | ● | ● | 2 | | | |
| Organizations & Societies | ● | ● | ● | ● | | ● | | | | ● | ● | ● |
| Government Agencies | | ● | | | | ● | | | | | | ● |
| Judicial decisions discussed | ● | ● | | | | | | | | ● | | ● |
| Large number of case citations | ● | ● | | | | | | | | | | |
| Case name index | ● | ● | | | | | | | | | | |
| Statutes cited & discussed | ● | ● | | | | | | | | ● | | ● |
| Statute index | ● | ● | | | | | | | | | | |
| Bibliographies | ● | ● | ● | 3 | | ● | ● | | | | | |
| Illustrations | | ● | | ● | ● | | ● | ● | ● | | | |
| Other Special Features | | | | 4 | 5 | 6 | 7 | ● | | | 8 | |

**1.** No separate biographies, but substantial biographical information within articles; names listed in index.

**2.** Under names of criminals.

**3.** Classified bibliography useful for works from first half of 20th century.

**4.** British emphasis.

**5.** Broad classified index includes headings such as types of crime, locations of crime, reporters, hideouts, crime studies, and wrongful convictions.

**6.** List of prison reform organizations; addresses of state planning agencies.

**7.** Classified index by type of murder; list of unsolved murders.

**8.** Separate list of foreign terms.

### What Encyclopedias Can Do for You

Here are some types of problems encyclopedias can help solve:

- You need to write or speak on probation, but don't know enough about the problems to *narrow the topic*. The series of articles called "Probation and Parole," in the *Encyclopedia of Crime and Justice* will help.
- Sutherland is one of the great names in criminology; a fast way to get at the basic outline of his ideas is through his *biography* in the *International Encyclopedia of the Social Sciences*; a shorter biography can be found in *The Concise Encyclopedia of Crime and Criminals*.
- You are a sociologist studying child abuse and need an *overview* of the problems involved in police search-and-seizure restrictions. You can get it from reading the article on "Search and Seizure" in either the *Guide to American Law* or *American Jurisprudence, 2d*.
- The book you are reading about gangs mentions the Swamp Angels, and you want to know who they are; you need to know when Willy Sutton died or what Omerta is; all of these can be found in *The Encyclopedia of American Crime*, by Carl Sifakis.

### History of Encyclopedias

Encyclopedias, conceived of as total compendiums of all knowledge, are more than two thousand years old. The most famous of the early compendiums is the work of the mid-eighteenth-century group of French thinkers called the Encyclopedists, who worked largely under the editorship of Denis Diderot. Probably the first truly modern encyclopedia, their thirty-five-volume work, with articles contributed by most of the leading thinkers of the period, was an attempt to encompass all the ideas and intellectual ferment of that era.

Following the pattern established by the Encyclopedists, the late eighteenth and nineteenth centuries continued to produce attempts at truly universal scholarly encyclopedias. One of the last such efforts, started in Germany in 1818, issued 167 volumes, completing only about half the alphabet before suspending publication in 1889.

The *Encyclopaedia Britannica*, inspired by Diderot's great French *Encyclopedie*, first appeared in Scotland in 1768. From that time until its eleventh edition, published in 1910–11, it too was an attempt at a scholarly compendium written for the highly educated minority. But with the increasing information flow from the newer fields in science, technology, and the social sciences, as well as the growth of scholarship in the more traditional subjects, it became clear to publishers that to encompass on a scholarly level all that was known about everything was an unattainable ideal.

Thus, today, the *Britannica*, the *Americana*, *Colliers*, and other encyclopedias with which you are familiar, rather than being compendiums of all that is known about the world, attempt only to summarize briefly the highlights. In addition, in response to rising rates of education and literacy, these encyclopedias are now written for the average adult rather than the scholar, with simpler versions such as the *World Book* and *Britannica Junior* prepared especially for children.

There are still, however, encyclopedias written for the serious student and scholar. As publishers realized that it was impossible to include all that was known about everything in one set of books, they also realized that encyclopedias could be produced which contained all that was most important about a single subject.

Probably the first such single-subject encyclopedia in English dealing with the social sciences was *The Encyclopedia of Social Reform, Including Political Economy, Political Science, Sociology, and Statistics, Covering Anarchism, Charities, Civil Service, Currency, Land and Legislation Reform, Penology, Socialism, Social Purity, Trades Unions, Woman Suffrage, Etc.* One thick volume, whose contributors included most of the leading social reformers of the day, it was first published in 1897.

The first large-scale modern encyclopedic treatment of the social sciences was the fifteen-volume *Encyclopedia of the Social Sciences,* published between 1930 and 1935. It was viewed universally as an outstanding scholarly achievement. That achievement was repeated and updated in 1968 with the publication of the seventeen-volume *International Encyclopedia of the Social Sciences*.

As earlier scholars found it necessary to divide universal knowledge into specializations, so by the mid-twentieth century, it became necessary to divide the specializations into subspecialities. Thus we now have separate encyclopedias for the various branches of the social sciences. These will be discussed later in this chapter.

### Types of Encyclopedia Articles

Encyclopedias contain two basic article styles: that which summarizes information, facts, or ideas and that which includes the origin and development of those ideas or facts. Almost all general encyclopedias and some subject encyclopedias are of the first type. Encyclopedias that are most useful for the serious researcher follow the second pattern. Since this distinction is important, the annotations below will alert you to those sets that include information on the development of concepts and ideas.

## USEFUL ENCYCLOPEDIAS FOR THE CRIMINAL JUSTICE RESEARCHER

The annotations below are in four groups:

1. An encyclopedia of primary importance to students of criminal justice;

2. Major subject encyclopedias in related fields;
3. Smaller encyclopedias and encyclopedic dictionaries;
4. Popular crime encyclopedias.

## The Major Encyclopedia for Criminal Justice

*Encyclopedia of Crime and Justice.* 4 vols. New York: Macmillan, 1983.

Students and researchers are fortunate to have this set available; its frequent use cannot be recommended too highly.

Articles are well written, authoritative, and frequently of substantial length. They discuss the history and development of ideas and movements in all areas of criminal justice as well as their current status. In an effort to include developmental, historical, and comparative aspects of the topics, many major areas are covered by a series of articles written by several experts. The value of the articles is further enhanced by considerable attention to legal precedent and citations to statutes and cases, a guide to legal citations, a glossary, a subject index to statutes and other legal documents, good bibliographies, and a very fine general subject index. There are no separate biographies, although there is considerable information about people within the articles.

No encyclopedia is designed to be read from cover to cover. This set, however, makes good browsing for those interested in criminal justice. A familiarity with the articles in this set would provide a good overview of the entire field.

## Major Encyclopedias in Related Fields

*International Encyclopedia of the Social Sciences.* 17 vols. New York: Macmillan and The Free Press, 1968.

Since publication this work has been viewed as a model subject encyclopedia, the single most important and encompassing publication for the social sciences. Written by acknowledged experts, it gives authoritative coverage to the fields of anthropology, economics, geography, history, law, political science, psychiatry, psychology, sociology, and statistics.

Published by the same firm which later produced the *Encyclopedia of Crime and Justice*, it is similar in format and approach to that publication. Because its emphasis was on the developmental aspects of the social sciences, it is still considered one of the most valuable sources for overviews and orientation to the social sciences, even though it is now somewhat dated.

*Encyclopedia of the Social Sciences.* 15 vols. New York: Macmillan, 1930–35.

Predecessor to the *International Encyclopedia of the Social Sciences*, this historic set is still valuable for the researcher.

*Guide to American Law.* 12 vols. St. Paul, MN: West, 1983–85.

This is the first multivolume encyclopedia of legal information for the lay person. The articles are accurate and well written although there is a variation in the depth of their coverage. Some articles are limited to definitions of terms; others are the short, fact-summary type usually found in general encyclopedias. Still others are long, analytical articles that could be very helpful in providing detailed background information on legal topics. The unusual arrangement of the encyclopedia may be somewhat confusing, for the long, analytical articles are printed on buff pages rather than the white paper of the rest of the encyclopedia and may duplicate topics covered in less detail in the white pages. The long articles include useful bibliographies.

Those who do not have ready access to a law library, or who want a completely nontechnical discussion of a legal topic, will find this source useful. Just be sure to check the buff pages as well as the white.

*American Jurisprudence, 2d.* Rochester, NY: Lawyers Co-op, 1962– . Updated by pocket parts.

*Corpus Juris Secundum.* St. Paul, MN: West, 1957– . Updated by pocket parts.

These are the two standard legal encyclopedias. The basic volumes of *Corpus Juris Secundum* are now so outdated that *American Jurisprudence, 2d* should be used if at all possible. In appearance both sets can be intimidating to the unfamiliar user, but most criminal justice students find these helpful sources well within their capabilities. Hints for their use are given in the chapter on legal resources.

*Encyclopedia of Psychology.* 4 vols. New York: John Wiley and Sons, 1984.

The importance of psychology in criminal justice research is obvious. Articles in this set are detailed, analytical, and thoroughly documented. They discuss the development of ideas and trends and key books and articles in their evolution. In the pattern made familiar by the *Encyclopedia of Crime and Justice*, large areas are divided into individual, related articles. Biographies of important psychologists, both living and dead, are included.

## One-Volume Encyclopedias in Criminal Justice

Scott, (Sir) Harold. *The Concise Encyclopedia of Crime and Criminals.* New York: Hawthorn Books, 1961.

A useful volume despite its age and lack of index. Some articles are quite extensive; most important movements and ideas are covered. The large number of biographies, unusual for their inclusion of lawyers, judges, and detectives, as well as criminals and criminologists, are particularly helpful.

Sifakis, Carl. *The Encyclopedia of American Crime.* New York: Facts on File, 1982.

This is the best of the one-volume encyclopedias. However, note that it is specifically concerned with crime and criminals. Coverage of psychological, sociological, and legal topics is minimal. Primary concerns are victims, criminals, and specific crimes and events. Also included are crime commissions, investigations, and specific prisons.

The index to this volume contains lists of articles under broad subject categories. These include individual cities and states, types of crime (such as assassinations or bombings), and other broad categories such as gangs, tongs, lynchings, unsolved murders, and wrongful convictions. These lists can be useful to the student looking for term-paper ideas and thought provoking to any researcher.

Williams, Vergil L. *Dictionary of American Penology*. Westport, CT: Greenwood Press, 1979.

More properly termed an encyclopedia, this one-volume compendium contains short articles on administrative and security problems, rehabilitative approaches, and significant historical trends and events. It is also very useful for the articles describing specific state prison systems and individual institutions.

### Popular Crime Encyclopedias

Gaute, J. H. H., and Robin Odel. *The Murderers' Who's Who: Outstanding International Cases from the Literature of Murder in the Last 150 Years*. New York: Methuen, 1979.

Gives a brief account of almost every famous murder case for the period covered. Includes bibliographies for each case. The classified index includes type of weapon, type of crime, and a list of unsolved crimes.

Nash, Jay Robert. *Almanac of World Crime*. Garden City, NY: Anchor Press/Doubleday, 1981.

Narrative descriptions of some of the world's most famous or bizarre crimes and criminals.

Nash, Jay Robert. *Bloodletters and Badmen: A Narrative Encyclopedia of American Criminals from the Pilgrims to the Present*. New York: M. Evans, 1973.

Nash, Jay Robert. *Look for the Woman: A Narrative Encyclopedia of Female Poisoners, Swindlers, and Spies from Elizabethan Times to the Present*. New York: M. Evans, 1981.

The subtitles tell all.

## DICTIONARIES

A specialized dictionary defines a word in its relationship to a specific body of knowledge. Although a word may have multiple meanings, the special dictionary takes it from its broader context and defines it in terms of a particular field. Changing nuances in the use of the word may be described, along with broader and narrower terms which help achieve an internal consistency of terminology within the field.

In addition to definitions, some specialized dictionaries include the type of information customarily found in encyclopedias: brief biographies, explanations of acronyms and abbreviations, and information about organizations and places.

The *Encyclopedia of Crime and Justice*, discussed above, includes a lengthy and very useful glossary of legal and criminal justice terminology.

Below are listed a few of the specialized dictionaries that are most useful to criminal justice researchers. There are others that deal with law, social science, drug use and abuse, psychology, and public administration. Ask your librarian to make a suggestion if you need one of these.

Black, Henry Campbell. *Black's Law Dictionary*. 5th ed. St. Paul, MN: West, 1979.

The standard legal dictionary.

Rush, George E. *Dictionary of Criminal Justice*. Boston: Holbrook Press, 1977.

This is the most generally useful of the special dictionaries in criminal justice because it reflects the multidisciplinary nature of the field. Definitions are moderately long.

De Sola, Ralph. *Crime Dictionary*. New York: Facts on File, 1982.

As the title indicates, the scope of this volume is not as broad as the one above—the most notable gaps being sociology and law. However, the definitions included are clear and sufficiently analytical to be very helpful. Among the more encyclopedic features are the inclusion of foreign terms, abbreviations, and acronyms; information on various terrorist groups and movements; and some biographies.

D'Auria, Michael M. *Legal Terms and Concepts in Criminal Justice*. Wayne, NJ: Avery Publishing Group, 1983.

Limited to legal terminology, this may be easier to use than a full legal dictionary.

SEARCH Group, Inc. *Dictionary of Criminal Justice Data Terminology: Terms and Definitions Proposed for Interstate and National Data Collection and Exchange*. 2nd ed. Washington, DC: U.S. Department of Justice, Bureau of Justice Statistics, 1981.

Strictly speaking, this is not a dictionary. It is a unique source dealing with a limited number of terms used in statistical compilations and reports within the criminal justice system (police, courts, corrections).

The purpose of this compilation is to improve the compatibility of statistics by recommending standardized definitions of terminology commonly used in statistical reports.

Entries can be a full page or longer. Varying meanings of the term will be discussed and recommendations given for its best use. In some cases, it is suggested that the term not be used at all.

*National Criminal Justice Thesaurus: Descriptors for Indexing Law Enforcement and Criminal Justice Information*. Washington, DC: U.S. Department of Justice, National Institute of Justice, 1984.

A thesaurus rather than a dictionary, this includes synonyms and broader and narrower terms for the entry word. Designed to be used in planning computer searches, it can also be helpful in compiling initial lists of terms to search in library catalogs or periodical indexes and abstracts.

## ANNUAL REVIEWS

Like encyclopedias, annual reviews provide overviews, but rather than synthesizing what is already known, they highlight the best in current research. Annual reviews may contain specially commissioned articles or a selection of recently published articles. They may attempt to cover many subjects in each issue or limit each to a single topic. Regardless of variations, however, annual reviews are always good sources for quality, up-to-date bibliographies.

*Criminal Law Review*. New York: Clark Boardman, 1979– .

Anthology of some of the most significant articles published during the preceding year. Each volume includes selections in the four areas of substantive criminal law, constitutional rights and remedies, trial and sentencing, and professional responsibility. Each year there is a very useful introductory survey of significant court decisions dealing with criminal law.

Morris, Norval, and Michael Tonry, eds. *Crime and Justice: An Annual Review of Research*. Chicago: University of Chicago Press, 1979– .

Commissioned essays discussing current research in all areas of criminal justice, with extensive bibliographies.

*Sage Annual Review of Studies in Deviance*. Beverly Hills, CA: Sage Publications, 1977– .

Different topics are covered each year. Samples are: "Law and Deviance," "Victims and Victimizers," "Crime and Deviance."

*Sage Criminal Justice System Annuals*. Beverly Hills, CA: Sage Publications, 1972– .

Different topics are covered each year. Samples are: "Drugs and the Criminal Justice System," "The Juvenile Justice System," "White Collar Crime," "Legal Rights of Prisoners."

# VI

# Newsletters, Newspapers, and News Broadcasts

## NEWSLETTERS

Newsletters are published primarily to convey current information to a group of readers with a common interest. Professional associations, corporations, government agencies, nonprofit organizations, and private publishers are among the groups which frequently publish newsletters.

Information contained in newsletters varies considerably: biographies of important people in the profession, notices of appointments to new jobs, employment listings, book reviews, notes on new or pending legislation and on recently decided cases, editorials, articles about recently awarded grants, research studies projected or currently underway, and notices of interim or final research reports. Most newsletter articles are brief.

Although not generally viewed by their publishers as research tools, we have seen in chapter II how important newsletters can be for the researcher. Not only do they contain information about the newest ideas and projects, but they have a more lasting value in those instances when a particular idea or study was not carried forward into a journal article or book.

*Criminal Justice Periodical Index* is the key to locating information in many of the newsletters of the criminal justice profession. Fortunately, it is an easy-to-use, straightforward, alphabetical subject index. Available online as well as in print form, it is discussed in detail in chapter VIII. Many valuable newsletters, however, are not included in *Criminal Justice Periodical Index*. The careful researcher may want to browse through some of these on a regular basis.

Because newsletters are designed for current awareness and not for research, some libraries will not subscribe to them; others will keep only the current issues. Where they are not available in a local library, they can be obtained on interlibrary loan.

Below is a list of newsletters selected to show the breadth of information and the variety of types and sources available.

### Criminal Justice

*Crime Control Digest: A Comprehensive Independent News Summary for the Law Enforcement Professional.* Washington, DC: Washington Crime News Service, 7620 Little River Turnpike, Annandale, VA. Weekly.

Includes news items and survey articles about court decisions, legislation, and publications.

*Criminal Justice Newsletter: An Independent Report on Significant Developments in Criminal Justice Policy and Administration.* New York: PaceCom Incorporated, 51 East 42 St. Formerly published by the National Council on Crime and Delinquency. Twice monthly.

Includes brief news notes, longer articles of summary and analysis, and regular columns on "Current Trends" and "Research Reports." Covers courts, corrections, law enforcement.

*Justice Assistance News.* Washington, DC: U.S. Government Printing Office. Ten times per year.

Published by the Office of Congressional and Public Affairs of the Office of Justice Assistance, Research, and Statistics, in conjunction with the Bureau of Justice Statistics, National Institute of Justice, and the Office of Juvenile Justice and Delinquency Prevention, news of these agencies and their activities and publications are covered.

### Police

*Law Enforcement News.* New York: Criminal Justice Center, 444 West 56 St. Monthly.

Newspaper format featuring news, comments, analyses, and research notes for law enforcement administrators.

*From the State Capitals: Police Administration: A Continuing Impartial Analysis of State and Municipal Legislative and Regulatory Trends of Nationwide Significance.* New Haven, CT: Wakeman/Walworth, Box 1939. Monthly.

Brief notes on legislative and administrative trends and developments of interest to police administrators.

*Police Labor Review.* Gaithersburg, MD: International Association of Chiefs of Police, Research and Development Division, 13 Firstfield Rd. Monthly.

Contains "synopsis of the latest developments in public sector labor relations both in and out of court," including contracts, legislation, and employment practices.

*Law Officers' Bulletin*. Washington, DC: Bureau of National Affairs, 1231 25 St., NW. Twenty-six times per year.

Discussions of recent federal and state legal decisions.

*Search & Seizure Bulletin*. Boston: Quinlan Publishing, 131 Beverly St. Monthly.

Original articles, summaries of articles appearing elsewhere, summaries and comments on federal and state court cases, all related to search and seizure.

### Corrections

*Corrections Digest: The Only Independent News Service for the Corrections Professional*. Washington, DC: Washington Crime News Service, 7620 Little River Turnpike, Annandale, VA. Biweekly.

Information on management techniques, training, rehabilitation concepts, trends, and programs from federal and state levels.

*Jail & Prisoner Law Bulletin*. South San Francisco, CA: Americans for Effective Law Enforcement (AELE), Legal Defense Center, 501 Grandview Drive. Monthly.

Summaries and short discussions of pertinent court decisions, federal and state.

*On the Line*. College Park, MD: American Correctional Association, 4321 Hartwick Rd. Monthly.

Newsletter of the Association.

## NEWSPAPERS

Newspapers are valuable sources of information for the criminal justice researcher. They can be used to study events or attitudes in a single place or to compare reactions to similar problems in different places. Regardless of the research topic, however, newspapers must always be used with great care. Although frequently described as objective and cited as primary sources there is always a degree of selectivity and subjectivity in the information presented. Someone decides which story to write, what to emphasize in the description of an event, whom to interview, and what parts of the interview to print.

With the above in mind, the criminal justice researcher can look to newspapers for a variety of kinds of information.

- Newspapers, like newsletters, contain announcements of research studies. Agencies anxious to publicize their activities may send press releases or hold press conferences to announce receipt of a grant, start of a project, or publication of an interim or final report.
- Newspapers reflect community attitudes. They are an outstanding source of information and opinion on topics such as police-community relations, public pressures for court reform, community response to placement of penal institutions, and political pressures on the criminal justice system.

- Newspapers obviously contain descriptions of events. They report what happened at the scene of the crime; who said what at the trial or at the city council meeting; eyewitness reports of the riot; and interviews with citizens, politicians, and police officials.

## Locating Newspaper Articles

Newspaper indexes were developed to keep the researcher from growing old or blind while looking for information in newspapers. A wide range of commercially prepared indexes is now available on microfiche, microfilm, and computer, as well as in print form. Your decision about which to use will be based on availability, coverage, and ease of use. The annotations below are arranged with the most useful and widely available sources first.

*National Newspaper Index*. Menlo Park, CA: Information Access Corporation, 1979– .

This is a combined subject index to all the articles in five different newspapers, cumulated for the past four years in one alphabetical arrangement. Thus, citations to a vast amount of newspaper information can be quickly and easily located. The newspapers currently covered are the *New York Times*, the *Christian Science Monitor*, the *Wall Street Journal*, the *Los Angeles Times*, and the *Washington Post*.

The *National Newspaper Index* is available in two formats: microfilm and online. The microfilm version, like the same company's *Magazine Index*, is stored in its own cabinet that looks somewhat like a small television set. The file is updated monthly. Unfortunately, the roll of film is not infinitely expandable, and older articles are shifted to microfiche supplements. Currently, four years are being maintained on the film cumulations, but this may change.

The online version has two files: *Newsearch*, updated daily for the most current information, and *National Newspaper Index* which is a duplicate of the microfilm version.

The ease of using *National Newspaper Index*, the fact that it always has the latest few years in one cumulation, and its currency make it a preferred source even when interested in only one of the included newspapers. It is important to remember that although started in 1979, it initially contained only the *New York Times*, the *Wall Street Journal*, and the *Christian Science Monitor*. The *Washington Post* and the *Los Angeles Times* were added in January 1983.

*Newsbank: Urban Affairs Library*. New Canaan, CT: Newsbank, Inc., 1977– .

This is a very useful combination of newspaper index and clipping service. The publishers subscribe to newspapers from over one hundred American cities. The papers selected are a fairly representative cross section of city, rural, and special interest papers, both dailies and weeklies. Significant articles are clipped from these papers.

There is a printed subject index to the collection; the articles themselves are on microfiche. A helpful feature of the subject index is the use of geographic subheadings.

*Editorials on File*. New York: Facts on File, 1970– .

Similar in concept to *Newsbank*, *Editorials on File* is limited to editorial material appearing in over 130 American and Canadian newspapers, for 98 different cities and counties.

*Editorials on File* comes in print form and reproduces by photo-offset the actual editorials that are selected. Issues come every two weeks, for insertion into a looseleaf binder. There is a table of contents on each biweekly issue. Indexes appear monthly and are cumulated quarterly.

*New York Times Index*. New York: New York Times, 1851– .

*Personal Name Index to the "New York Times Index," 1851–1975*. Succasunna, NJ: Roxbury Data Interface, 1977; and *Supplement, 1975–79*. Verdi, NV: Roxbury Data Interface, 1984.

Although a New York City newspaper, coverage in the *New York Times* has always been national in scope. Generally considered one of the nation's best newspapers, both microfilm copies of the paper and its printed index are widely available.

Published continuously since 1851, printed indexes have been made for the paper from volume 1, no. 1.

The *Personal Name Index to the "New York Times Index"* lists in one alphabet all personal names in the *New York Times Index*, from 1851 to 1975, with a supplement covering 1975–1979. Since almost all newspaper stories involve at least one person, this is an invaluable tool. Use it when you know the name of a person involved but are not sure of the year of the event, or use it to trace stories which developed over a period of years.

Easiest online access to the *New York Times* is through the *National Newspaper Index*.

*Official Washington Post Index*. 1972– .

The first ten years of the published indexes to the *Washington Post* are somewhat difficult to use, but since 1982 typography has improved and very useful geographical subdivisions have been added for most subjects.

The *Washington Post* index is available online in its own file from 1979 to date and as part of the *National Newspaper Index* since 1983.

*Wall Street Journal Index*. 1955– .

Although seemingly written for a limited audience, the *Wall Street Journal* is very highly regarded by scholars and researchers in many fields. It has a truly national viewpoint. Coverage of criminal justice–related topics is considerably more extensive than the paper's name implies. It is a particularly good source for infor mation about white-collar crime and organized crime. Each issue of the index is divided into two sections: "Corporate News" and "General News." Information related to crime is most often in the "General News" section.

Published indexes are available to many other newspapers including the *Chicago Tribune*, *Cincinnati Enquirer*, *Denver Post*, *Detroit News*, *Los Angeles Times*, *Minneapolis Tribune*, *New Orleans Times-Picayune*, and the *San Francisco Chronicle*. Information from newspapers of smaller circulation frequently can be accessed through unpublished indexes and clipping files prepared by the newspaper itself, a library, or an historical society. Consult your librarian for leads to these.

Very useful lists of commercial and noncommercial indexes to a wide variety of American newspapers can be found in:

Milner, Anita Cheek. *Newspaper Indexes: A Location and Subject Guide for Researchers*. 3 vols. Metuchen, NJ: Scarecrow Press, 1977–82.

### Paperless Newspapers

Recent years have seen the growth of a phenomenon which is equally marvelous and expensive: complete newspapers available through a computer terminal.

These "paperless-newspaper" data bases provide not only index terms but the complete text of every article in the newspaper. Among the most useful of these services are the *New York Times Full Text*, which makes that paper available from 1981 on, and *NEXIS* which provides access to eight wire services and all the leading news magazines, as well as four newspapers (including the *New York Times* and the *Washington Post*). These services are expensive and must be subscribed to on an individual basis.

An ever-increasing number of newspapers of local interest are now also becoming available through total online systems. Vu-text Information Systems, a Philadelphia company which is the major vendor of these papers, now provides online, full-text access to more than two dozen newspapers, including the *Sacramento Bee*, the *Miami Herald*, the *Philadelphia Inquirer*, the *Anchorage Daily News*, and the *Wichita Eagle-Beacon*.

All full-text services are expensive. They are more likely to be available in corporate or agency libraries, where ease and speed of access are prime considerations, than in academic or research libraries where cost is more likely to be a factor.

## NEWS BROADCASTS

Much of today's news is communicated through broadcast media rather than newsprint. Anyone who regularly watches network news programs knows how much coverage is given to topics of interest to criminal justice researchers. Thus, the two sources below are of interest:

*CBS News Television News Broadcasts*. Glen Rock, NJ: Microfilming Corporation of America, 1975– . Microfiche.

*CBS News Index: Key to the Television Broadcasts*. Ann Arbor, MI: Microfilming Corporation of America, 1975– .

This set consists of microfiche copies of television scripts and printed subject indexes to the microfiche. The indexes are issued quarterly and cumulated annually. Some libraries purchase only the indexes and rely on interlibrary loan to obtain copies of the scripts.

Both public affairs programs and hard news items are put on fiche and indexed. Included are the CBS network morning and evening news programs, *CBS Special Reports*, *Face the Nation*, *Sixty Minutes*, and various other CBS news programs.

Although this is a very rich source of information about current topics in criminal justice, you may have to search a bit to locate stories on specific topics, since the indexing is somewhat broad. For example, a discussion of graffiti is listed under crime but not under the more specific graffiti. If there is a person associated with the event you are researching, it is best to start with the personal name rather than the subject.

*Television News Index and Abstracts: A Guide to the Videotape Collection of the Network Evening News Programs in the Vanderbilt Television News Archive.* Nashville, TN: Vanderbilt University Library, 1968– .

This is a special occasion source. Rather than filmed copies of the scripts, these are videotapes of the actual news broadcasts. Included are the evening news programs of the three major networks: ABC, CBS, and NBC. The tapes are available on interlibrary loan from Vanderbilt University. You can request either an entire broadcast as shown or an edited compilation of a series of items from several different newscasts. There are varying charges depending on the amount and format of the tape needed.

The abstracts are fairly detailed, specifying what was shown as well as what was said, and include the names of people who can be heard as well as seen.

The *Television News Index and Abstracts* is issued monthly but has no cumulations. If you are interested in television coverage of an event but are uncertain of the month or year in which it occurred, use the *National Newspaper Index* or the *New York Times Index* to ascertain the date.

# VII

# Documents, Reports, and Conference Proceedings

For the purpose of this chapter we will talk about reports and government documents as though they are distinct entities. Government documents are publications issued or authorized by any office of a legally organized government. Reports are records (1) of an organization or group; (2) of research results; (3) of research in progress; or (4) of other technical studies. Proceedings are collections of reports and papers presented at conferences. In actuality, a government document can be a report and a report can be a government document. The main concern is not in the definition but rather in locating the specific document or report that will best contribute to your research. Most sources discussed in this chapter will not deal exclusively with criminal justice subjects; they are, however, important sources of criminal justice information.

## GOVERNMENT DOCUMENTS

Documents can be issued by governments at any level: federal, state, regional, county, municipal, intergovernmental, or international. Access to them is as varied as the sources from which they emerge.

### Federal Documents

Federal documents are found in every format noted in the information flow from the listing of raw data by the Bureau of the Census to the *Police* volume, issued by the National Advisory Committee on Criminal Justice and Goals. Documents containing raw data are considered primary sources; documents interpreting that data are secondary sources. In a single year, the United States Government Printing Office prints thousands of titles in paper and in microfiche. To assure that this wealth of material is available to its citizens, the Superintendent of Documents sends free copies of these items to almost fourteen hundred depository libraries throughout the country. Other libraries will buy the items they need.

Early in your research, therefore, it is advisable to master the intricacies of utilizing federal documents. This sheer mass of material, emanating from a variety of federal agencies, assures the coverage of a broad spectrum of topics. Business, economics, political science, social science, public administration, law, criminal justice, statistics, psychology—all are subjects within the purview of federal documents.

Libraries include government documents in their collections in three ways: (1) they catalog them and integrate them into the regular collection; (2) they do not catalog them but put them in a separate section with its own access tools; and (3) they do a combination of (1) and (2).

If the library adds documents to its regular collection, you will find them by consulting the library's catalogs. Smaller libraries that are not depositories are more likely to do this.

In libraries that have a separate government documents collection, you will find the items arranged by the Superintendent of Documents (SuDocs) system rather than the Dewey or LC classification systems. SuDocs call numbers arrange documents by the agency that issues them. Thus, items on the same subject are not necessarily shelved together. Studies on violence done by a presidential commission, for instance, will be shelved with the commission's publications. Studies on violence completed by the National Institute of Justice will be in an entirely different location.

### *Guides to Federal Documents*

*The United States Government Manual*. Washington, DC: U.S. Government Printing Office, 1935– . Annual.

If the plethora of government agencies tends to discourage or confuse you, take time out to look at this manual. It provides succinct descriptions of the agencies of all three branches of the government. Published annually, it clarifies the history and structure of each agency as well as the interaction among agencies.

There often is no catalog, in the usual sense, to materials arranged by SuDocs classification. There are, fortunately, a number of effective printed and online indexes which function as catalogs. The *Monthly Catalog of United States Publications*, issued continuously since 1895 in book format but with varying titles, is your most inclusive access tool.

*Monthly Catalog of United States Publications*. Washington, DC: U.S. Government Printing Office, 1895– . Monthly.

Whatever nasty stories you may have heard about the *Monthly Catalog*, they are no longer true. There are now multiple indexes: author, title, subject, key words from titles, series/reports and stock numbers. Monthly indexes are cumulated semi-annually and annually. From all the access points you can find the entry number for the item you need and then its call number. The indexes prior to 1974 may be intimidating; ask for help.

Commercial publishers are now issuing in microformat a cumulative edition of the *Monthly Catalog* that includes all entries since 1976.

Online, the *Monthly Catalog* may be searched through *BRS* and *Dialog*. A government-issued data base, it is less expensive than commercial ones. Coverage starts with 1971 entries and will be more current in the data base than in its printed counterpart.

*Cumulative Subject Index to the Monthly Catalog of United States Government Publications, 1900–1971*. 15 vols. Washington, DC: Carrollton Press, 1973.

*Cumulative Title Index to the United States Public Documents, 1789–1976*. 16 vols. Arlington, VA: United States Historical Documents Institute, 1982.

Let these two cumulations do the work for you. Decades of documents can be accessed by a single search.

*GPO Sales Publications Reference File (PRF)*. Washington, DC: U.S. Government Printing Office, 1974– . Six updates per year.

This microfiche listing includes currently available, forthcoming, and recently out-of-stock government publications. Intended as a tool to help order documents, it can be used as a current-awareness source. Since many documents go out of print quickly, and are dropped from the *PRF*, it should be used in conjunction with other available access tools. It is indexed by subject, title, and keywords and phrases.

*CIS/Annual: Index to Congressional Publications and Public Laws*. Washington, DC: Congressional Information Service, 1970– . Monthly.

Rare indeed is a subject or issue that sooner or later is not discussed in Congress. This excellent resource indexes all publications of the U.S. Congress except the *Congressional Record*. Hearings, prints, documents, reports, public laws—all are noted in an index volume and described in detail in an abstract volume. Testimony and supporting documents supplied by witnesses at hearings are included. So detailed are the abstracts that they not only summarize the document but actually index its contents, giving you page numbers on which specific information appears.

*CIS/Index* has annual and four- or five-year cumulations. Documents indexed in *CIS/Annual* are available on microfiche, giving patrons instant access to the material. If your library does not purchase the entire set, it can easily obtain the fiche you need, either by interlibrary loan or by direct purchase. CIS promises twenty-four-hour turnaround time on orders. Ease of use plus quick and sane access to the documents make this set a pleasure for the researcher.

Available online through *Dialog* and *SDC*, *CIS* can prove costly to search because of the detailed entries. A knowledgeable searcher can help control such costs. The indexes to this set are so good, however, that online searching may not prove significantly better than manual searching.

*American Statistics Index*. Washington, DC: Congressional Information Service, 1974– . Monthly.

Another treasure. See chapter X for details.

*Index to U.S. Government Periodicals*. Chicago: Infordata International, 1970– . Quarterly.

While the *Monthly Catalog* will give you titles of government periodicals, this tool indexes substantive articles of lasting research and reference value appearing within over two hundred periodicals published by the US government. It tends to include items missed by nongovernmental indexes that pick up articles from only the major government periodicals. Use it in conjunction with other periodical indexes.

*Public Affairs Information Service Bulletin*. New York: Public Affairs Information Service, 1915– . Semimonthly.

This classic alphabetical subject index, discussed in detail in chapter VIII, includes documents. It cumulates quarterly and annually. Available online since 1976 through *Dialog* and *BRS*.

Only if you need to do exhaustive or retrospective research in federal documents will you use these additional tools. Ask your librarian for help with the following standard sources:

Poore, Ben Perley. *A Descriptive Catalogue of the Government Publications of the United States*. Reprint. Washington, DC: U.S. Government Printing Office, 1885. New York: Johnson Reprint, 1970.

Covers September 5, 1774 to March 4, 1881.

Ames, John Griffith. *Comprehensive Index to the Publications of the United States Government, 1881 to 1893*. 1905. Reprint. New York: Johnson Reprint, 1962.

*Documents Catalog*. Washington, DC: U.S. Government Printing Office, 1893. Reprint. New York: Johnson Reprint, 1963.

Covers 1893 to 1940. Overlaps *Monthly Catalog*.

Andriot, John. *Guide to U.S. Government Publications*. McLean, VA: Documents Index, 1973– . Vol. 1 published annually.

Compendium of lists of serials, periodicals, and irregular publications issued by governmental agencies. Valuable for tracing agency changes; contains elusive titles.

### International Documents

Access to international documents is discussed in chapter XIV.

### State Documents

Access to state documents is much more nebulous than access to federal documents. No exhaustive index exists to help you find publications issued by state, county, or local governments. Within each state a state library may serve as the depository for state and local documents. If so, a visit to that library will enable you to assess its potential for research. Some state libraries or state historical societies also produce indexes to their state's publications. The fastest way to find out if your state's publications are indexed is to check with your librarian. Persistence is an asset in tracking down documents issued below the federal government level. Limited aid is furnished by the following publications.

### *Guides to State Documents*

*Statistical Reference Index*. Washington, DC: Congressional Information Service, 1980– . Monthly.

This is your very best bet because it includes many reports at the state level. Even if you are interested in discussion and not statistics, remember that most documents contain some statistics. Those which do, even if mainly narrative, are picked up here. Fast to use; good abstracts. See chapter X for further information.

*The Monthly Checklist of State Publications*. Library of Congress. Washington, DC: U.S. Government Printing Office, 1910– .

You may have to wait for the annual subject index to find this checklist really useful. The monthly issues only list by state and agency those documents received by the Library of Congress from state agencies, associations of state agencies, and regional organizations. The annual subject index includes topics such as arrest, corrections, delinquents, parole, prisons, prosecution, recidivists, and victims of crime. The index pulls together under each state name all entry numbers for documents received from that state, so you can do comparative studies across states by subject and single state studies under state name.

*State Government Research Checklist*. Lexington, KY: Council of State Governments, 1947– . Bimonthly.

Particularly useful if you know state legislatures are researching certain topics, such as drunken driving or ombudsmen. This publication lists and briefly abstracts research reports issued at the state level, whether by legislative service agencies, state study commissions and committees, intergovernmental groups, or university bureaus of government. Index cumulated in February issue.

*Recent Publications on Governmental Problems*. Chicago: Merriam Center Library, 1932– . Monthly.

Concentrating on the field of public administration, this monthly guide lists under broad subject areas books, government documents, public and private agency publications, and articles from eight hundred journals. Bail, drugs, and juvenile delinquency are examples of subjects noted. Not cumulated.

*National Directory of State Agencies*. Arlington, VA: Information Resource Press. Biennial.

We include this directory because it gives you names and addresses of contact persons in state agencies of each state. It first lists under each state its agencies, then lists under service area (corrections, court administration, police) those agencies in all states. Great for use if you are doing a survey and need personal or agency names to contact.

## County and Municipal Documents

If your area has a county, municipal, or regional reference library, be sure to use it. The library may be part of a public library or may be in a governmental office. Your research may require a visit to a specific governmental unit. Call ahead, make an appointment. The contact person may need time to pull together the items or information you need.

### *Guides to County and Municipal Documents*

Koehler, Cortus T. *A Practitioner's Guide to Information Sources and the Literature on County Government: An Annotated Bibliography*. Sacramento, CA: County Supervisors' Association of California, 1983.

Books, articles, documents, reports, periodicals, and even court cases are cited in this overall view of material on county government, finance, and services. Stresses the practitioner's viewpoint.

*Index to Current Urban Documents*. Westport, CT: Greenwood Press, 1972– . Quarterly.

Easy-to-use access tool for documents from almost three hundred cities or counties. It includes hundreds of police department annual reports and special reports on particular problems such as riot control, public relations, rape, police ethics, and violence. Subject and geographic indexes, cumulated annually, note the documents, most of which are available on microfiche. If your library does not purchase the fiche set which accompanies this index, use interlibrary loan.

*Municipal Government Reference Sources*. Edited by Peter Hernon et al. for the ALA Government Documents Round Table. New York: R. R. Bowker, 1978.

Helpful, but dated. This is a good introduction to the types of publications municipalities are apt to publish and to their often nebulous availability.

## Regional and Intergovernmental Documents

You may find documents from regional and intergovernmental agencies indexed in any one of the indexes discussed throughout this chapter. If the federal government is involved, check the federal sources. If local government is involved, check the same tools that index state, county, or municipal sources. Be aware that such documents have a tendency to fall through the cracks. A call or visit to the regional or intergovernmental agency may be your most effective research avenue.

## REPORTS

When we look at our definition of reports, we can certainly anticipate a problem in accessing them. We said that reports are records of an organization or group, of research results, of research in progress, or of other technical studies. As such, they can fall within every stage of the information flow and within any format from an unpublished manuscript to a bound book to a multivolume set. Reports can be primary sources if they present findings or secondary sources if they interpret the findings. Reports cover a broad spectrum of topics from methodology to statistics to evaluation.

Note that many sources that index reports recognize the difficulty of obtaining the documents once you have identified them. Hence, these companies or agencies not only index reports but also make available the actual documents, usually on microfiche. As you work, note those sources.

We have already discussed some excellent leads to reports: *Monthly Catalog of United States Government Publications*, *American Statistics Index*, and *Statistical Reference Index*. There are other sources to explore. Be reminded again: many of these do not deal exclusively with criminal justice subjects but are viable sources of criminal justice information. Note that in some cases we are dealing with organizations that provide information and not just access tools.

### Access to Reports

*Criminal Justice/NCCD*. John Cotton Dana Library, Rutgers University, 185 University Avenue, Newark, NJ 07102.

Rutgers University has acquired the library of the National Council on Crime and Delinquency (NCCD), renaming it the Criminal Justice/NCCD Collection. Founded in 1909, the nonprofit NCCD concerned itself with all manifestations of crime. Its library grew over the years to include periodicals, newspaper clippings, state and federal documents, dissertations, studies, monographs, and published and unpublished reports.

The reports in this collection are probably its most valuable contribution, since they are less likely to be available through other sources. Over three thousand of these noncopyrighted items, many subfederal government reports, have been microfilmed and indexed by a printed guide, *Crime and Juvenile Delinquency*. If your library owns this microfiche collection, utilize it for its unique contributions. If not, borrow the material on interlibrary loan. Other aspects of the NCCD collection and its access appear in chapter VIII.

*National Criminal Justice Reference Service (NCJRS) Library*. Box 6000, Rockville, MD 20850.

Reports, books, documents, audiovisual resources, and journal articles comprise the eighty thousand–plus collection housed at NCJRS, a program of the National Institute of Justice. Again it is the reports and document segment of this collection that is of primary interest, since the periodical articles and books can be located through other sources. This collection should always be used when doing research on criminal justice subjects. Arson, prison crowding, crime prevention, victim services, abuse of power, and organized crime are only a handful of the topics included.

Actually a national and international clearing house, NCJRS disperses its criminal justice information by means of interlibrary loan and document distribution in both paper copy and on microfiche. About 25 percent of the collection is available on microfiche, free in limited quantities, otherwise by purchase. The NCJRS collection is indexed by the *Document Retrieval Index*, the *Cummulative Index to NCJRS Microfiche Collection, #1-93,999,* and the online *NCJRS* database.

*Document Retrieval Index*. Washington, DC: National Criminal Justice Reference Service, 1972– . Annual.

NCJRS provides access to its entire collection via this index on microfiche, with the basic 1972–1978 set supplemented by annual updates. Subject, title, and personal name indexes lead to citations arranged by NCJ numbers. Whether or not your library purchases the microfiche collection, it should still make available this index.

*Cummulative Index to NCJRS Microfiche Collection, #1-93,999*. Rockville, MD: NCJRS, 1984– .

Indexes only the microfiche portion of the collection. Will be updated by supplements.

*NCJRS*.

Available from Dialog, this is the major machine-readable index exclusively devoted to criminal justice information. Indexes the entire NCJRS collection. Its cost is reasonable and its updating promised monthly. This is good news for researchers who have had to put up with too long a lag time in the past. A thesaurus of indexing terms, revised annually, is available in both printed and microfiche formats.

*National Technical Information Service (NTIS)*. 5285 Port Royal Road, Springfield, VA 22161.

The word technical can be misleading. Many of the half million reports dispersed by NTIS are in the field of behavioral and social sciences. Government-sponsored research mushroomed during the post–World War II era. Since these particular research reports were not published by the federal government, they did not usually find their way into the pages of the *Monthly Catalog*. Those few which did were identified by an "@" sign. In 1970, the National Technical Information Service was established to distribute on a cost recovery basis, in either paper or microfiche, the federally sponsored research reports of federal agencies, their contractors, and their grantees. NTIS has since become a central source of federally generated, machine-processable data files. Online searches and prepackaged bibliographies, titled "Published Searches," have been added to the services offered. Some state and local governments are now contributing their reports to the data bank. Access to NTIS reports is available through a published index and its online versions.

*Government Reports Announcements and Index*. Springfield, VA: National Technical Information Service, 1964– . Semimonthly.

Don't let this multivolume annual index intimidate you. Sections are by keyword, personal author, corporate author, contract/grant number, and NTIS order/report number. Criminal justice reports appear in groups titled "History," "Law and Political Science," "Psychology," and "Sociology." Remember that NTIS files include reports of completed research. Keywords will be your best approach for criminal justice subjects. The online version of this index, titled *NTIS*, is updated biweekly and is available through *BRS*, *Dialog*, and *SDC*.

*The Rand Corporation*. 1700 Main Street, Santa Monica, CA 90406.

With a staff of almost one thousand persons, evenly divided between researchers and support personnel, the nonprofit Rand Corporation easily qualifies as one of the primary research centers in the country. Concentrating on military and security matters between 1946 and 1964, the corporation has broadened its scope to include social issues of national and international scope. Its Institute for Civil Justice analyzes policy and planning in law enforcement and its Graduate Institute confers degrees in public policy. Research findings are reported in books and published series entitled "Reports," "Notes," "Papers," and the discontinued "Research Memorandum." Some Rand materials appear in such indexes as *Government Reports Announcements and Index* and *Scientific and Technical Aerospace Reports*, but the primary index is *Selected Rand Abstracts*.

*Selected Rand Abstracts: A Quarterly Guide to Publications of the Rand Corporation*. Santa Monica, CA: Rand Corporation, 1963. Quarterly.

Current unclassified publications of the corporation are indexed by subject and by author, with an abstract section providing succinct summaries. Each issue is cumulative, with the December issue covering the entire year. Entries appear under common terms, such as courts, crime, criminal justice, and prisons, but concentrate on concepts such as decision making, policy analysis, and planning.

*Smithsonian Science Information Exchange (SSIE)*. Room 300, 1730 M St., NW, Washington, DC 20036.

SSIE was started in 1949 to exchange information on medical research. Its coverage now includes the social sciences. Note that this service deals with research in progress. There is usually little or no overlap between NTIS and SSIE materials. About 10 percent of SSIE information is from private and nonprofit sources outside the government. SSIE information is available from *BRS*, *Dialog*, and *SDC*. No print version is available.

*Dialog* uses two data bases to access SSIE materials: (1) *SSIE Current Research*, a closed data base covering research initiated or completed during 1978–1982; and (2) *Federal Research in Progress*, which provides information on ongoing, federally funded research projects.

Data base records of *Federal Research in Progress* include title, principal investigator, performing organization, sponsoring organization, level of funding, and a description of the research. Research completed during the past two years is included. Criminology and law and legal procedures are covered. Such data bases provide leads to published literature, unpublished reports, and white papers. (White papers are authoritative, usually biased, statements on an issue of public policy and are written to influence opinion.)

### Access to Subject-Specific Reports

*Drug Use and Abuse* is included as a pioneer example of a genre of needed access tools in the field of criminal justice. Such a review compiles the report literature available on a specific subject. Well prepared, this innovative guide should be emulated by similar reviews of reports in other subject areas.

Austin, Gregory A., and Michael L. Prendergast. *Drug Use and Abuse: A Guide to Research Findings. Vol. 1, Adults; vol. 2, Adolescents*. Santa Barbara, CA: ABC-Clio Information Services, 1984.

Each volume is self-contained. Volumes summarize and index in detail the findings of 238 federally funded studies completed between 1970 and 1980 on the psychosocial aspects of drug use and abuse. Abstracts are lengthy and grouped alphabetically by author under topics. The abstracts include purpose, operational definitions, findings, and conclusions. Indexes are by author, topic, drug, sample type, sex, age, ethnicity, location, methodology, and instrument.

### Major Criminal Justice Commission Reports

Special mention should be made of reports generated by government commissions established to investigate a specific aspect of criminal justice. These are indexed by the *Monthly Catalog* at the federal level and by the various sources mentioned at other governmental levels. Major commission reports are noted in Appendix C.

## CONFERENCE PROCEEDINGS

Conference proceedings appear at an early stage within the flow of criminal justice information. Conferences are often the locus for movement of ideas into the formal information network. During conferences new ideas can be shared, societal issues aired, and buzzwords born. You may first hear about a conference report from someone who attended the conference or a professional associate. As the news travels from one person to another, however, titles tend to become garbled and conferences confused. The following sources will help track down a conference paper.

### Guides to Conference Papers and Proceedings

*Association Journals*.

Conference papers often appear in issues of the journals published by the association sponsoring the conference. Check these out as a possible source.

*Sociological Abstracts (SA)*. San Diego, CA: Sociological Abstracts, 1952– . Five issues per year.

*Sociological Abstracts* includes in each issue a section of conference paper abstracts. *SA* is published five times a year with annual cumulated indexes. Useful for delinquency, public opinion, human relations aspects of criminal justice, and research methodology. Available online through *Dialog*. Further information can be found in chapter VIII.

*Index to Social Science and Humanities Proceedings (ISSHP)*. Philadelphia, PA: Institute for Scientific Information, 1979– . Quarterly.

*ISSHP* includes the "most significant published proceedings." This keyword index provides entry and page numbers leading to conference information. Helpful because it lists paper titles, presenters, and their institutions. Category index lists conference by broad subject areas, including "Criminology and Penology" and "Law." Also has sponsor index, author/editor index, meeting location index, corporate index, and geographic and organization section.

*Bibliographic Guide to Conference Publications*. Boston: G. K. Hall, 1975– . Annual.

This guide includes conference publications cataloged during the past year by the Research Libraries of the New York Public Library and the Library of Congress. Covers all countries, all languages. Indexes are by subject as well as author, title, group, and conference name. An authoritative source for researchers.

*Directory of Published Proceedings. Series SSH-Social Sciences/Humanities*. Harrison, NY: InterDok, 1968– . Quarterly.

The citations are entered chronologically by year and month, and the indexes, cumulated annually, are by editor, location, and subject/sponsor. No listing of papers presented.

*Index of Conference Proceedings Received*. Boston Spa, England: The British Library Lending Division, 1973– . Monthly.

A keyword index to almost two hundred thousand conference proceedings held by the British Library Lending Division. Monthly with annual, five-year, ten-year, and eighteen-year cumulations. It includes all subject fields, with emphasis on technical conferences. Its online counterpart is *Conference Proceedings Index*, available only from the British vendor *BLAISE-LINE*.

*Proceedings in Print*. Arlington, MA: Proceedings in Print, 1964– . Bimonthly.

Alphabetical listing of proceedings already in print of conferences, symposia, lecture series, congresses, hearings, seminars, courses, institutes, colloquia, meetings, and published symposia. Listing followed by subject and group index. Also lists proceedings which will never be published, thereby saving the researcher's time. Annual cumulative index. Leans toward the technical.

# VIII

# Indexes and Abstracts

Other than librarians, your best friends in the library may prove to be indexes and abstracts. An index is an alphabetical list of names, places, or topics discussed in a publication. An abstract, as the term is used in this chapter, adds a further dimension. It functions as an index but also presents a brief summary of the important points of the document or file. Although as a group they are referred to as periodical indexes and abstracts, many are not limited to periodicals but include reports, documents, and even books in their coverage. You may also hear them called indexing and abstracting services.

You will recall the location of articles in the information flow discussed in chapter II. Indexes and abstracts provide the earliest truly systematic access to information as it is revealed in current literature.

## KINDS OF INFORMATION SOURCES

In the discussion of information flow, the differentiation was made between three kinds of information sources: those designed for popular consumption, those designed for the professional, and those aimed at the scholar. You may, at times, want to utilize information designed for any one or all of these target audiences. Much depends on the nature of your research. If you are writing on the methodology of team policing you may well utilize professional journals; on the public's reaction to it, popular magazines; on the concept and theory of team policing, scholarly journals. Remember it is the accuracy of the information that is your chief concern.

Indexes may reference popular, scholarly, or professional journals or a combination of these. They may cover multiple subject areas or may be limited to a particular discipline. Even though indexes devoted to criminal justice will be your primary resources, keep in mind that this is an interdisciplinary field. Thus, indexes designed for related areas will be of great utility. You may, for instance, turn to business indexes for personnel research, to psychological indexes for deviance, to educational indexes for juvenile delinquency, and to public affairs indexes for public sector administration.

## STRATEGIES FOR USING INDEXES AND ABSTRACTS

Indexes are usually arranged alphabetically by subject. Abstracts tend to be set up under broad subject areas, with a detailed subject index in the back. Such an arrangement is called a classified index or abstract. Both indexes and abstracts include all the bibliographic information needed to identify and locate the item. Be sure to copy all information down, exactly the way it appears in the citation. If an index or abstract uses abbreviations, do not assume you know for what they stand. Look them up in the abbreviations table in the front or back of the volume. Journal titles are often disconcertingly similar, and it is vital to have the exact, full title.

Indexes usually cumulate their entries, sometimes quarterly and then annually or for a specific number of years. Abstracts usually cumulate their indexes in the same manner. If you need the most current citations, use the most current issues first; if somewhat older information will suffice, save time by using the more inclusive cumulations first.

A thesaurus may accompany an index. This is a list of subject headings under which the specific publication indexes items. If the index you choose does not have a thesaurus, you will need to compile your own list of all possible terms under which relevant information might be indexed. Do not assume that all indexes use the same terms—they do not. That is why we reiterate the advice to keep a record of each source you use and a list of subject headings useful in that source. Although each index will be consistent in the subject headings it uses, not every relevant heading will appear in each issue of that index.

In addition to entry by subject, some indexes and abstracts also index by authors, geographic locations, reviews, and other features.

If you are interested in documents and reports as well as periodical articles, pay special attention to those sources which include them.

## CRIMINAL JUSTICE INDEXES AND ABSTRACTS

*Criminal Justice Abstracts* (CJA). (Formerly *Abstracts on Crime and Delinquency* and *Crime and Delinquency Literature*.) Monsey, NY: Willow Tree, 1968– . Quarterly.

Descriptive abstracts in *CJA* note a publication's contents, including research findings, methods, and conclusions. Selective coverage, based on editorial evaluation, pulls items from professional journals, books, dissertations, and reports from research institutions, governmental agencies, and private organizations. Arrangement is classified under such topics as "Crime and the Offender," "Organized Crime," "Corrections," and "Related Social Issues." The subject and geographic indexes are cumulated annually; in earlier years an asterisk by an entry indicated a research study. Useful literature review articles in each issue deal with such aspects of criminal justice as police, use of deadly force, domestic violence, and political crime. Formerly published by the National Council on Crime and Delinquency. Available on microfilm.

Additional abstracts from the National Council on Crime and Delinquency, not include in *CJA*, are available on microfilm and indexed by the printed *Index to Abstracts on Crime and Juvenile Delinquency*, now issued by University Microfilms International. Further information on NCCD appears in chapter VII.

*Criminal Justice Periodical Index*. Ann Arbor, MI: University Microfilms International, 1975– . Three issues per year.

General criminal justice coverage, including security, appears in this easy-to-use alphabetical index to over one hundred journals. Its two sections include an author index and a subject index based on LC subject headings supplemented by special topics and cross references. The inclusion of professional newsletters enhances its value for charting current developments. Unique subject entries list book, film, and periodical reviews. Especially valuable are the entries under "Reports," since clues to locating such documents often prove elusive elsewhere. Available online: *Dialog*. Has thesaurus.

*Criminology and Penology Abstracts, (CPA)*. (Formerly *Excerpta Criminologica* and *Abstracts on Criminology and Penology*.) Amsterdam: Kugler Publications, 1961– . Bimonthly.

Published in the Netherlands, this scholarly abstract is international in scope. Its classified arrangement covers "the etiology of crime and juvenile delinquency, the control and treatment of offenders, criminal procedure, and the administration of justice." Entries tend to stress the theoretical and conceptual treatment of subjects. Includes foreign-language materials. Author/subject index in each issue, cumulated annually. Prior to 1973 it included topics on police science and forensics. Also available on microfiche.

*Police Science Abstracts*. (Formerly *Abstracts on Police Science*.) Amsterdam: Kugler Publications, 1973– . Bimonthly.

A 1973 spin-off of *Criminology and Penology Abstracts,* this title gives international coverage of police science and forensic science and medicine. Arrangement and format duplicate *CPA*. Necessary for any research involving police science. Available on microfiche.

*NCJRS* (online database).

*Document Retrieval Index* (*DRI*). Rockville, MD: National Criminal Justice Reference Service, 1972– . Annual.

Both these indexes reflect the contents of the library of the National Criminal

Justice Reference Service. *NCJRS* is the online version, available from *Dialog*. Has thesaurus.

*DRI* is an example of the new breed of indexes: one produced only on microfiche. Because over 50 percent of the *NCJRS* and *DRI* entries are government documents and reports, we included a discussion of NCJRS and its access tools in chapter VII. Another 10 percent index monographs, proceedings, and theses; 6 percent films and audiovisual material; 31 percent is devoted to index entries for journal articles. The 250 periodical titles covered are 95 percent English-language publications. Consider this coverage and use accordingly, certainly in conjunction with other indexes.

*Forensic Science Abstracts: The International Medical Abstracting Services*. Amsterdam: Elsevier Science Publishers, 1975. Ten issues per year.

One of the forty-four abstract journals extracted from *Excerpta Medica*. It is arranged by subject for current awareness and has a detailed table of contents and author and subject indexes. Coverage includes crime scene investigation, child abuse, sex offenses, and medically related criminal justice studies. Useful to medical examiners, coroners, police and criminal investigators. Best coverage available for this subject. Available online: *BRS*, *Dialog*. Available as part of *Excerpta Medica* (*Emed* or *Embase*). Has thesaurus.

*Law Enforcement and Criminal Justice Information Database*. Eagan, MN: International Research and Evaluation, 1954– . Quarterly updates.

This is an online data base, unusual because it is available not through any commercial vendor but only through direct subscription from the producer. This is not a well-known source. It merges information from the National Technical Information Service and the National Criminal Justice Reference Service with other materials to note crime prevention, forensics, criminology, equipment, and the criminal justice system.

## USEFUL INDEXES IN RELATED AREAS

### General Coverage

*Current Contents: Social and Behavioral Sciences*. Philadelphia, PA: Institute for Scientific Information, 1969– . Weekly.

*Current Contents* is a valuable tool to use for the social sciences. It reprints the tables of contents of selected periodicals as they are published. This allows you to browse through one thousand three hundred journals published worldwide and books as they are published. Not every journal, of course, appears in every issue. Sections cover sociology, social issues, psychology, law, and management. Indexing is by keywords in the titles of articles. Includes an author index and directory of publishers' addresses.

*Social Science Citation Index* (*SSCI*). Philadelphia, PA: Institute for Scientific Information, 1969– . Quarterly.

An exciting and challenging index. Don't be put off by its tiny print and multiple volumes. *SSCI* covers 250 books per year, approximately 1,500 of the most frequently cited international journals in the social sciences in toto and another 2,800 selectively. It includes related materials from the natural, physical, and biomedical sciences. The fourth issue each year is the annual cumulation, and there are five-year cumulations. *SSCI* divides into four indexes.

1. *Citation Index*

Use this if you know the name of an author and want to see how often that author's articles are being used as references by other authors. Remember that the cited author's article could have been published during any previous year. The articles citing that author have been published during the year covered by the index. In alphabetical order it lists the author cited, followed by the source of the cited article(s), the citing author, and the citing source. The first section of the *Citation Index* gives cited personal authors, the second cited corporate authors, and the third lists cited anonymous articles arranged by the journals in which the articles appeared.

2. *Corporate Index*

The *Corporate Index* consists of two sections: geographic and organization. In the geographic section the authors are listed under the state and city, or country, in which the author's organization or institution is located. The title of the item is given and, if an article, its location. If you want to see which members of a faculty have published during a specific year, look under its state and city for the college's name. The faculty names and book or article citations will appear. The organization (or institution) section tells you where an organization is located and you can then check the geographic section for authors and their publications. You will probably use the *Corporate Index* less frequently than the others.

3. *Source Index*

This is actually the list of authors of all books and articles indexed in each year's *SSCI* set. Anonymous articles are listed in a separate section under the name of the journal in which the article appeared. Each entry under an author's name gives the bibliographic information for that item: its full title, type of item, journal title in which it appeared, volume, issue, pages, year. For chapter and book entries the information includes author, edition, chapter or book title, publication year, page numbers for chapters, and a book identification number which is found in the volume in a "List of Books Covered." In addition, under each author's name you will find a list of references cited—authors, journal, year, volume, and page. When you find an article useful to your research, be sure to check the references the author used. They may be equally helpful.

4. *Permuterm Subject Index*

All significant words in an author's title are indexed and paired with a second word in the title. This provides a keyword index with the added bonus of picking up and indexing under new terms in a field. The buzzwords appear here long before they become standard subject headings. The disadvantages are that the index uses only words in authors' titles and you must look under variant forms of the word and also under related words, such as juvenile, juveniles, youth, and youthful. Authors' names are listed under the keywords and must then be looked up in the

*Source Index* in order to find the full bibliographic information for the article. Available online: *BRS*, *Dialog*, *SDC*. Note that the online version is updated weekly. Easier to use online but can be expensive if you print out the full citations online. Check with your librarian about the best way to search *SSCI*.

*Social Sciences Index*. (Formerly *International Index to Periodicals*, 1907–1965; *Social Sciences and Humanities Index*, 1965–1973.) New York: H. W. Wilson, 1974– . Quarterly.

An alphabetical author and subject index to over three hundred periodicals, it cumulates annually. Easy to use, it indexes journals of a scholarly nature and proves valuable for its interdisciplinary coverage of the social sciences. Indexes book reviews. Available online: *Wilsonline*.

*Dissertation Abstracts International* (*DAI*). Ann Arbor, MI: University Microfilms International, 1861– . Monthly.

Cumulated indexes in print make it possible to check in a single source for all dissertations completed from 1861 to 1972. Annual five-year and one-year cumulations supplement these. Searching all these years online is a great time saver. The keyword index identifies dissertations covering specific topics. Author index included. Part A covers the humanities and social sciences; Part B, the sciences and engineering; Part C, since 1977, European abstracts. An essential resource for those contemplating a doctoral degree. Available online: *BRS*, *Dialog*, *SDC*. The online version searches keywords not only in the titles but also in the abstracts. In addition, *DAI* accesses entries in *Master's Abstracts*, an index to theses from a limited number of cooperating universities.

## Coverage in Specific Fields

### *Law*

*Current Law Index* (*CLI*). Belmont, CA: Information Access Company, 1980– . Monthly.

A committee of law librarians chooses the seven hundred law periodicals and national legal newspapers to be indexed. Citations are to key English-language law and law-related literature, including articles, reviews, commentaries, monographs, and government publications. Covers material from the United States, Canada, England, Australia, and New Zealand. Book reviewers assign grades of A to F to books reviewed. With quarterly and annual cumulations, it indexes under subject, author/title, cases, and statutes, including state and foreign. *CLI* is available in printed copy and as part of the microfilm and online *Legal Resources Index*, whose additional materials include newsletters. Available online: *Dialog* (*Legal Resources Index*).

*Index to Legal Periodicals*. New York: H. W. Wilson, 1908– . Monthly.

An alphabetical subject index covering English-language legal journals from the United States, Canada, Great Britain, Ireland, Australia, and New Zealand. Salient feature, since 1917, is the "Table of Cases Referred to in Articles." Also includes statutes tables and index to book reviews. Yearbooks, annual reviews, and annual institutes are indexed. Definitely an easy-to-use index. Many of the journals covered are published by law colleges. Cumulated quarterly and annually. Available online: *Wilsonline*.

*KINDEX: An Index to Legal Periodical Literature Concerning Children*. Pittsburgh, PA: National Center for Juvenile Justice, 1965– . Semiannual.

The main volume covers 1965 to 1975, with semiannual supplements and annual cumulations. Concerned with youth and the criminal justice system, it is arranged by broad subject area. Indexes four hundred English-language periodicals by subject, geographic location, court cases involved, and author. Includes such topics as child abuse, juvenile delinquency, and law and legislation affecting children and youth.

*Legal Resources Index*.

See *Current Law Index*.

### *Psychology*

*Psychological Abstracts*. Washington, DC: American Psychological Association, 1927– . Monthly.

Abstracts in classified arrangement provide nonevaluative summaries of the world's literature in psychology and other behavioral sciences. Every criminal justice researcher, at some time, will need to consult this important research tool. Good for personnel and training issues, applied psychology, and causes and effects of criminal behavior. Citations are to journal articles, books, reports, and dissertations (until 1980). A *Thesaurus of Psychological Terms* provides subject headings. There are author and subject cumulated indexes. Available online: *BRS*, *Dialog*, *SDC*. The online version, available from 1967, includes dissertations. Has thesaurus.

### *Sociology and Social Work*

*Sociological Abstracts*. San Diego, CA: Sociological Abstracts, Inc., 1952– . Five issues a year.

Covers the international literature of sociology, including criminology. Abstracts are nonevaluative. Arranged by topics, one important section for criminal justice information is titled "Sociology of Law." A separate section in each issue covers papers presented at a major sociological conference. The indexing under various forms of a term may prove confusing at first. Probably easier to use online. Available online: *BRS*, *Dialog*.

*Social Work Research and Abstracts*. (Formerly *Abstracts for Social Workers*.) New York: National Association of Social Workers, 1965– . Quarterly.

Combines coverage of books and journal literature in the field with reports of original research. Useful for such topics as rehabilitation, probation, drugs, dropouts, and parole. Of interest to both practitioners and researchers. Indexes are by author and title and cumulate annually.

*Human Resources Abstracts* (*HRA*). (Formerly *Poverty and Human Resources Abstracts*.) Beverly Hills, CA: Sage Publications, 1966– . Quarterly.

A useful index for researching the relationship of poverty and unemployment to crime and delinquency. Items, indexed under Library of Congress subject headings, include English-language periodicals, books, reports, and proceedings. *HRA* is organized by broad subject categories and cumulates its author and subject indexes annually.

### *Education*

*ERIC* (online data base).

*Resources in Education*. Washington, DC: U.S. Department of Education, 1966– Monthly.

Especially good for delinquency, crime and the schools, and correctional education, this source indexes a microfiche collection of educational research reports, curriculum materials, and other education-related items. Monthly, semiannual, and annual indexes. A thesaurus provides indexing terms. Most documents indexed are available on microfiche. Available online: *BRS*, *Dialog*, *SDC*. Has thesaurus. The online version includes both *ERIC* documents and journal entries from *Current Index to Journals in Education*.

### *Business*

*ABI/Inform*. Louisville, KY: Data Courier, 1971– . Monthly.

This business data base concentrates on administration and management, including public administration. As such it provides valuable leads to substantive journal articles. Surprisingly effective for criminal justice topics. No printed counterpart. Available online: *BRS*, *Dialog*, *SDC*. Has thesaurus.

*Business Periodicals Index*. New York: H. W. Wilson, 1958– . Monthly.

Subjects other than business range from "Crime and Criminals" to "Strikes–Police." An obvious source for articles on corporate crime. Also valuable for administration, personnel, and management materials. Indexes over 275 English-language periodical titles and has a separate book review section. Easy to use alphabetical subject arrangement with quarterly and annual indexes. Available online: *Wilsonline*.

*Business Publications Index and Abstracts* (*BPIA*). Northbrook, IL: Management Contents, 1980– . Monthly.

Usually a printed index or abstract is converted to machine-readable form and becomes an online data base. In this case the online data base *Management Contents* has become a printed index. *BPIA* is produced in two volumes: one an author and subject index; the other abstracts. The index to books, periodicals, proceedings, and transactions is cumulated quarterly; there is an annual cumulation. All standard criminal justice subject headings are used: courts, crime and criminals, prisons, criminal procedure, criminal law, and white-collar crime. Covers public sector administration and management. Available online: *BRS*, *Dialog*, *SDC* (*Management Contents*). Has thesaurus.

### *Public Administration*

*Public Affairs Information Service Bulletin (PAIS)*. New York: Public Affairs Information Service, 1915– . Semimonthly.

Valuable for information on criminal justice administration, public policy, current issues, and municipal functions. This alphabetical subject guide to social science literature indexes periodicals, books, and pamphlets and is especially helpful in locating documents. Quarterly cumulations and annual cumulations with author index. Available online: *BRS*, *Dialog*. Has thesaurus. Online version includes the *PAIS Foreign Language Index*, and articles tend to be indexed under more subject headings than in the printed version.

*Sage Urban Studies Abstracts*. Beverly Hills, CA: Sage Publications, 1973– . Quarterly.

Indexes speeches and legislative research as well as English-language journal articles, documents, and books. Covers such subjects as courts, crime, criminal justice, plea bargaining and is particularly good for planning. Entries are classified and indexed by author and Library of Congress subject headings. Indexes cumulate annually.

*Urban Affairs Abstracts*. Washington, DC: National League of Cities, 1972– . Weekly.

Excellent coverage of up-to-date relevant urban literature. Includes among its 550 periodical titles some Canadian and foreign publications as well as U.S. publications. Indexes less-widely circulated journals specializing in municipal affairs. Its classified entries have author and geographic indexes. Semiannual and annual cumulations include the abstract section, subject description, author index, geographic index, and source list.

### *History*

*America: History and Life*. Santa Barbara, CA: American Bibliographical Center–Clio Press, 1964-- . Three issues per year.

Published in four parts: A. Article Abstracts and Citations, B. Index to Book Reviews, C. American History Bibliography, and D. Annual Index. Includes U.S. and Canadian history from prehistoric times to the present. Indexes periodicals published in forty-two languages in ninety countries, but all abstracts are in English. Use it for retrospective studies and for social history and popular culture relative to criminal justice. Tends to be scholarly. Available online: *Dialog*.

## Coverage of Specific Groups

*Child Abuse and Neglect*. Washington, DC: National Center on Child Abuse and Neglect, 1965– . Annual.

Sections of this online data base of interest to criminal justice researchers include its abstracts of published documents, court decisions, and excerpts of current state statutes. Coverage discusses social and economic factors and policy making. Parts of the data base are updated semiannually, the rest annually. Available online: *Dialog*.

*Sage Family Studies Abstracts*. Beverly Hills, CA: Sage Publications, 1979– . Quarterly.

Includes international, English-language, professional information gleaned from articles, books, pamphlets, reports, proceedings, documents, and even speeches. Delinquency, deviance, and abuse, within the framework of the family, are discussed. Uses Library of Congress subject headings. Author and subject headings to entries, arranged under broad categories, are cumulated annually.

*Sage Race Relations Abstracts*. Beverly Hills, CA: Sage Publications, 1976– . Quarterly.

These abstracts cover police, courts, crime, delinquency, and the judiciary from the viewpoint of racial concerns. Abstracts from three hundred-plus periodicals, books, and reports are arranged under broad subject headings. Coverage is worldwide but in English. Indexes by author and subject cumulate annually.

*Women Studies Abstracts*. Rush, NY: Rush Publishing Company, 1972– . Quarterly.

Includes the impact on and the influence of women in the areas of criminal justice and criminology. Entries by broad subject areas are culled from international, but English-language, periodicals, books, and reports. Subject indexes are cumulated annually.

### Coverage of Popular Sources

*Readers' Guide to Periodical Literature*. New York: H. W. Wilson, 1900– . Semimonthly.

Don't overlook this as a source for current hot topics, which often appear in the popular literature first. Since it indexes magazines written for the layman, it often provides articles with good basic facts. This alphabetical index to authors and subjects is cumulated quarterly and annually. A separate section cites book reviews. Available online: *Wilsonline*.

*Magazine Index*. Menlo Park, CA: Information Access, 1977– . Monthly.

An alphabetical index on microfilm, this notes articles in general or popular magazines published in the United States and Canada. Since the entries cumulate on one film it saves looking through individual volumes for each year covered. Indexing is based on Library of Congress subject headings with supplemental terms. Entries appear under author, subject, and named persons. Since coverage is general, use it critically. Available online: *Dialog*.

*Magazine Index ASAP*. Menlo Park, CA: Information Access, 1984– . Monthly.

"ASAP" (as soon as possible) in the title announces that this data base will print out an entire article either online or off. It indexes and searches every word of the text of articles appearing in over fifty popular magazines as well as a dozen or so federal and international periodicals. Coverage begins with January 1983 issues. Some entries appear within three weeks of publication, making it a great current-awareness tool. *Magazine Index ASAP* is a harbinger of technology's increasing contributions to timely information access. Available only online: *Dialog*.

# IX

# The Library Catalog

You are undoubtedly familiar with the single most important tool in the library: the catalog. Regardless of its form the modern library catalog enables you to know: 1. Whether the library owns a particular book; 2. All the books the library owns by a particular author; 3. All the books the library owns about a particular subject. For purposes of this discussion we will assume that the catalog includes only books, but documents, recordings, tapes, items in microformat, and titles of periodicals might also be included.

## A BIT OF HISTORY

Libraries have always attempted to maintain records of what they owned. The earliest such records were not catalogs in the sense in which we know that term, but were just lists, sometimes arranged in broad subject areas, but more commonly arranged by author or title.

By the nineteenth century most of these lists were kept in large ledger books with separate sections for each letter of the alphabet. Books were entered over a period of time as the need arose and thus were only roughly alphabetical.

In the late nineteenth century, a system evolved of putting information about the books onto individual cards so that new acquisitions could easily be put in proper alphabetical order, and, thereby, a semblance of order was achieved.

Until the twentieth century, authors were the only element that was consistently listed in library lists or catalogs; titles were included only occasionally and subjects not at all. Because the quantity of material available was so much more limited than today, scholars were able to work with these limitations.

The earliest attempts to provide information about the subjects of books came in the form of entering the book in the ledger by catchword title, with the informative word first, such as "Convicts, the value of solitary confinement for" or "Prisoners, the isolation of."

The type of consistent subject approach with which we are now familiar did not become really feasible until after the publication of uniform lists of subject headings by the Library of Congress early in this century.

## THE CATALOG TODAY

Forms of catalogs have continued to evolve. Mid-twentieth-century developments in computer technology and micropublication have greatly influenced the format of the modern catalog. Thirty years ago almost every library in the country had a card catalog. Today, readers of this book may be using a catalog on cards, in computer-printed book form, on computer-printed microfiche, or through a computer terminal and CRT (cathode-ray tube) screen. Regardless of the format, the same basic principles of organization and use apply.

When using the library catalog, be alert and be careful. If you have any trouble, or do not find exactly what you need, ask the librarian for help. Library catalogs, in any format, are more complex than they may appear.

As we have said, every item entered in the catalog has three potential access points: author, title, and subject.

## LOCATING BOOKS BY AUTHOR

Obviously, books have to be written or edited by people. Whether living or dead, if the last name is known, the author can be located through the catalog. When two or three people are jointly responsible for the book, they will all be listed. Where there are more than three authors, only the first will be listed in the catalog.

The problem with authors and the catalog comes about when the person who physically does the writing is not considered to have ultimate responsibility for the work but only to be the facilitator—the one who puts onto paper the ideas, concepts, and facts arrived at by a group of people. In such cases, the group, most often people employed by a private or government agency or by a corporation, is considered the author of the work. Authors such as the Subcommittee on Constitutional Rights of the Senate Committee on the Judiciary, the Police Foundation, or the Chicago Police Department are sometimes difficult to locate in the catalog.

The best advice in such cases is:

1. If the item has a distinctive title, such as *Challenge of Crime in a Free Society*, and not just "Report," look it up under the title;
2. If the item comes from a private agency, like the Police Foundation, look directly under the name of the agency;
3. If the item comes from a city, state, or federal government agency or committee, look under the name of jurisdiction first, then, look for the specific agency or committee.

## LOCATING BOOKS BY TITLE

The most important thing to know when locating books by title is to ignore "the," "a," and "an" at the beginning of a title but not in the middle. With the exception of the three articles when used as the first word, every word in the title counts in alphabetizing. If there are abbreviations, numbers, or symbols anywhere in the title, be wary; there are several different ways of filing these elements.

## LOCATING BOOKS BY SUBJECT

(Note: Appendix A contains selected lists of Library of Congress subject headings related to criminal justice studies.)

In order to make the most effective use of the subject approach to the catalog, there are two concepts which need to be understood: (1) the concept of specific entry and (2) the concept of subdivisions, both subject and geographic.

### The Concept of Specific Entry

Specific entry means that each book is given the most specific subject heading (or headings) which accurately describes the book. This principle makes it possible to locate easily entries for works on narrow subjects by providing subject headings such as a "Police patrol." However, a book is not given both specific and general headings; if it is listed under "Police patrol," it will not also be found under "Police." Always try to find the most specific heading first. If there is not enough material listed under the specific heading, move on to the more general heading. Other examples of looking under specific rather than general headings are: "Bank robberies" rather than the broader "Robbery"; "Uxoricide" (wife murder) rather than "Murder"; "Afro-American prisoners" rather than the broader "Prisoners"; "Alcoholism and crime" rather than either "Crime" or "Alcoholism." There are two major disadvantages to specific entry. First, most people tend to think initially in general terms, and it takes both discipline and experience to reorient your thinking. Second, even when we do think in specific terms, it is sometimes hard to know the exact terminology that has been chosen by the Library of Congress (witness "Crimes aboard buses," "Children of women prisoners," or "Aeronautics in police work.") Although cross-references are generally supplied, they are not always in the place you look. If you are not sure that you have located the most relevant subject heading, check with the librarian.

## The Concepts of Subject and Geographic Subdivision

### *Subject Subdivision*

For subtle grammatical reasons some specific terminology is given as a *subdivision* of a broader subject rather than as a separate phrase. A dash (–) between the subject and some smaller aspect of the subject indicates a subdivision. Some of the most useful subdivisions are used for every subject in the catalog; examples of these are: –Bibliography, –Encyclopedias, –Directories, –History, –Research, –Study and teaching. Other subdivisions apply only to specific subjects; examples are: Police–Response time, Crime prevention–Citizen participation.

### *Geographic Subdivision*

When a book deals with one or two specific countries or states, the subject headings describing the book will have a geographical subdivision. For example: Police–Great Britain, Correctional institutions–Sweden, Prisoners–Michigan, and Murder–California. The examples above are limited to countries and states, because the rules about cities are in a state of flux. They exemplify the fact that the library catalog is not static, and even the most experienced library user sometimes needs the help of the librarian. At the moment, the following may all exist in any one library catalog:

1. Detroit–Police;
2. Police–Michigan–Detroit;
3. Police–England–London;
4. Police–New York City.

Example one is the old method; the name of the city appears first. Examples two and three are the currently recommended practice; the subject appears first, then the country or state, then the city. Example four illustrates one of the four cities which are exceptions to the current rules. The four cities are: (1) New York City, because of size; (2) Washington, DC, because there is no state; and (3) Berlin and (4) Jerusalem, because of complex political reasons. Be aware that most libraries are making no attempt to convert the older forms of entry to current practice. If you want information about a city, in most cases it would be wise to look under both the city name and the subject. Cross-references may or may not be supplied between the two.

## FILING

Whether the library catalog is in card, book, fiche, or computer format there are two common types of arrangements: (1) authors, titles, and subjects interfiled in one alphabet; this is called a dictionary catalog; and (2) authors and titles in one alphabet with subjects in a separate alphabet; this is, for obvious reasons, called a divided catalog. In some places, there is a third division, with titles being separated from authors.

You may have thought that you mastered the basic principles of alphabetization way back in grade school. Alas, libraries can be more complicated than just B after A, BE after BC, and so on. When the need is to alphabetize a variety of formats, such as phrases, single words, phrases with subdivisions, names, and places, principles of alphabetization go well beyond grade school simplicity. They are not the same in every library or even in every catalog in the same library.

There are two different ways entries can be alphabetized within each of the catalog types: (1) Strictly alphabetical, ignoring both punctuation and logic. Almost all catalogs that are arranged by computer are filed this way; some manually filed catalogs also use this system. (2) Mostly alphabetical, with logic applied to the sequences and punctuation affecting the arrangement. Below are examples of the strictly alphabetical and the alphabetical/logical for both a dictionary catalog and the subject section of a divided catalog.

### DICTIONARY CATALOG

| Strictly Alphabetical | Alphabetical/Logical |
|---|---|
| POLICE (subject) | Police, John (author) |
| POLICE–ACCIDENTS (subject with subdivision) | Police and you (title) |
| POLICE ADMINISTRATION (subject in phrase form) | Police roundup (title) |
| Police and you (title) | POLICE (subject) |
| Police Foundation (corporate author) | POLICE–ACCIDENTS (subject with subdivision) |
| POLICE–ITALY (subject with geographic subdivision) | POLICE–SUICIDAL BEHAVIOR |
| Police, John (author) | POLICE–ITALY (subject with geographic subdivision) |
| POLICE PROFESSIONALISM (subject, in phrase form) | POLICE–SOUTH DAKOTA |
| Police Roundup (title) | POLICE ADMINISTRATION (subject in phrase form) |
| POLICE–SOUTH DAKOTA | POLICE AND MASS MEDIA |
| POLICE–SUICIDAL BEHAVIOR | POLICE AND PROFESSIONALISM |

**SUBJECT SECTION OF A DIVIDED CATALOG**

| **Strictly Alphabetical** | **Alphabetical/Logical** |
|---|---|
| POLICE | POLICE |
| POLICE–ACCIDENTS | POLICE–ACCIDENTS (subject subdivision) |
| POLICE ADMINISTRATION | POLICE–SUICIDAL BEHAVIOR |
| POLICE–ITALY | POLICE–ITALY (geographical subdivision) |
| POLICE PROFESSIONALISM | POLICE–SOUTH DAKOTA |
| POLICE–SOUTH DAKOTA | POLICE ADMINISTRATION (phrase) |
| POLICE–SUICIDAL BEHAVIOR | POLICE PROFESSIONALISM |

## MULTIPLE CATALOGS IN THE SAME LIBRARY

Most libraries have in recent years made attempts to update technologically their cataloging procedures and catalog formats. In most cases it was not considered economically feasible to convert all of the old records to the new formats. Thus it is common to find a closed catalog of cards containing material cataloged before a certain date (generally sometime in the 1970's) and a new catalog, in either book, fiche, or computer format, containing material added to the collection after that date. Where there is more than one catalog the researcher needs to be aware of the differences and, in many cases, use each one. Note that the dividing date between them is generally when the material was cataloged by the library, not when it was initially published, and that in some cases items still in the old format are gradually being moved into the new catalog. Be alert to the possibility of different filing arrangements in each catalog.

## PUBLISHED AND ONLINE CATALOGS OF OTHER LIBRARIES

In this age of computers, computer printing, and microphotography, it is possible to consult the catalogs of geographically distant libraries without ever leaving home. You might find the following interesting.

Cambridge University. Institute of Criminology. *The Catalogue of the Radzinowicz Library*. 6 vols. Boston: G. K. Hall, 1979.

The arrangement of this catalog is different from those with which most Americans are familiar. Reduced-size reproductions of cards from the card catalog of this famous criminology library are arranged according to the Bliss classification scheme (a rival to the Library of Congress system). It is worth the time orienting yourself to the system if you are particularly interested in problems of British police and crime. The catalog is not limited to books but includes pamphlets, reports, and, particularly for the earlier periods, individual periodical articles.

Los Angeles Public Library. Municipal Reference Library. *Catalog of the Police Library of the Los Angeles Public Library*. 2 vols. Boston: G. K. Hall, 1972. *Supplement*. 2 vols. 1980.

Although now somewhat dated, this catalog of one of the oldest police libraries in the United States is still useful. Like the catalog of the Radzinowicz library, it includes reports, pamphlets, and individual periodical articles as well as books. The inclusion of periodical articles for the period prior to the publication of standard periodical indexes for police material makes this source particularly important for historical work.

*OCLC (Ohio Computerized Library Center).*

Started in the late 1960's, this is an electronic data base which now contains more than eleven million records of books and serials owned by over four thousand American and Canadian libraries. An OCLC terminal provides instant access to the catalogs of these libraries. The data base provides complete bibliographic information and tells you which of the participating libraries own the book. Many libraries can place interlibrary loan requests directly through the OCLC terminal.

Previously available only to members utilizing special equipment and commands, most of the bibliographic information in the OCLC data base may now be accessed through BRS in the same fashion as other data bases.

*RLIN (Research Libraries Information Network).*

Similar to OCLC but with membership limited to the largest research libraries in the country.

# X

# Statistics

Statistics can add zest to any report. With them you can compare, contrast, evaluate, illustrate, analyze, summarize, impress, communicate, clarify, and even mystify.

Statistics touch everyone's lives, from the student checking credit hours to the police captain utilizing a sophisticated computer for calculating victimization within a designated urban area, age, and ethnic population. One can easily feel inundated by the abundance of available statistics or totally frustrated by the lack of that one figure needed to substantiate a hypothesis.

## STATISTICS DEFINED

Statistics have been collected for centuries. The word statistics has its origin in the word state, implying a systematic compilation and study of demographic and political facts. Facts so collected were used for political purposes, often taxation. Mary and Joseph went to Bethlehem to be "counted." William the Conqueror listed both inhabitants and animals for his 1068 *Domesday Book*. London officials in 1532 noted the number of dying citizens and their diseases. Since numbers were involved in these early compilations, the word statistics evolved to mean the assembly and analysis of numbers.

Science, as a discipline, afforded statistics credibility by recognizing it as a branch of applied mathematics. In the twentieth century, statistics have played a major role in the research of the sciences, the social sciences, and even the humanities. Over the last three decades, computers, with their rapid and efficient calculations, have increased the use of statistics by making them easier to manipulate and analyze.

When we use the word *statistics* we need to define our thrust. Statistics can mean: (1) the numbers or numerical facts collected and (2) the methods used to analyze such numbers and to draw conclusions. This chapter will concentrate on the location and use of compiled statistics. It will not deal with methods of statistical analysis.

## CRIMINAL JUSTICE STATISTICS

Criminal justice statistics emanate from a variety of sources. The FBI, the Bureau of the Census, the Bureau of Justice Statistics, and the Administrative Office of the U.S. Courts are all among the federal agencies that collect and disseminate criminal justice statistics. Statistical Analysis Centers have been established in each state to coordinate work in criminal justice statistics. Added to these sources are thousands of state and local agencies, research centers, academic units, and professional organizations that collect, analyze, disseminate, and use criminal justice data.

Statistics thus compiled are used by lawmakers, public administrators, law enforcement personnel, correctional officers, the media, the public, researchers, and students. Among other things, statistics are used to validate planning and budgeting decisions and for evaluation and projections.

Your research may require finding and using many statistics or only a very few. Regardless of the number, those you use must be creditable, appropriate, and applicable to your topic and easily interpretable by your intended audience. Be wary of using statistics from varying sources. Time periods may not be consistent, terms may be defined differently, and sources may vary in quality and comprehensiveness. Know and cite the source of every statistic you use.

Some statistics are easy to locate in readily available sources such as an almanac. Others may prove elusive. Fortunately, there are finding guides that arrange and cite statistics by subjects, compilations of statistics to use, and organizations to contact that collect statistics.

## FINDING GUIDES FOR STATISTICS

Finding guides for statistics indicate what statistics are available, where they may be found, and what subjects they cover. Thus it is not as necessary to remember specific sources as it is to know that these resources will guide you to the statistics you need.

*American Statistics Index (ASI)*. Washington, DC: Congressional Information Service, 1974– . Monthly.

*Index to International Statistics (IIS)*. Washington, DC: Congressional Information Service, 1983– . Monthly.

*Statistical Reference Index (SRI).* Washington, DC: Congressional Information Service 1980– . Monthly.

This triad mitigates many concerns researchers have about locating statistics. Because they are general statistical indexes, you use them for diverse disciplines. Note, however, that they include subjects vital to criminal justice research. Each title identifies publications within its parameters, classifies them by their source, and indexes and summarizes their contents. Each index is accompanied by a collection in microfiche of all or part of the documents it indexes.

Different and definitive groups of sources are covered by each index. *ASI* extracts statistical information located in publications of the federal government. *IIS* does the same for publications of international organizations. *SRI* concentrates on U.S. sources other than the federal government. These include trade, professional, and nonprofit organizations and institutions; business organizations; commercial publishers; independent research centers; state government agencies; and university research centers. *SRI* does include some data on foreign countries when published by these groups.

All three titles are published monthly, with quarterly, annual, and multiple-year cumulations. Each issue has two parts: an abstract and an index. Start with the index. Look in the subject index under "crime and criminals." In addition to entries on that topic you will find a "see also" list. These are other topics used in the index. Reading this list will give you a good idea of the criminal justice topics covered in each set. *ASI*, *IIS*, and *SRI* all have specialized indexes following the general subject index. These help you refine your subject by breaking down information into geographic, economic, or demographic categories.

A number following the subject in the index volume leads to a succinct synopsis of that item in the abstract volume. The actual pages of the cited document are given where the specific information or tables appear. The abstracts are a marvelous time saver since they are frequently informative enough for you to decide whether or not the item will be useful for your research. Since microfiche collections of materials indexed are available for all three titles, you have access to the information immediately. If your library purchases only the index and not the fiche, use interlibrary loan. We cannot stress too strongly the research value of *ASI*, *IIS*, and *SRI*. Of the three, *American Statistics Index* is available online through *Dialog* and *Orbit*. It seems safe to assume *IIS* and *SRI* will follow suit.

Manheim, Jarel B., and Allison Ondrasik. *Data Map: Index of Published Tables of Statistical Data, 1984.* 2nd ed. New York: Longman, 1984.

Ten thousand tables of statistical data from twenty-eight sources are indexed by subject, table, and source in this computer-generated index. Of the sources, seventeen are U.S. government publications, six are U.N., and five are private or public organizations which publish data. Smaller libraries may tend to own this research tool, rather than *ASI*, since the sources it indexes are readily available.

*Statistics Sources: A Subject Guide to Data on Industrial, Business, Social, Educational, Financial and Other Topics for the United States and Internationally*. Edited by Paul Wasserman, et al. 9th ed. Detroit, MI: Gale Research, 1984.

A selective and annotated bibliography of key statistical sources, this index uses such subject headings as courts, crime and criminals, and law enforcement. Citations included lean heavily toward federal publications. An interesting feature is the list of machine-readable data bases.

## CRIMINAL JUSTICE STATISTICS COMPILATIONS

*National Crime Surveys: Criminal Victimization in the U.S.* Bureau of Justice Statistics. Washington, DC: U.S. Government Printing Office, 1973– .

Based on surveys by the Census Bureau to provide data for longitudinal studies, these reports reflect incidents of rape, robbery, assault, larceny, burglary, and auto theft. Note that this series covers the victimization aspects of crime and does not necessarily reflect just reported crimes.

*National Prisoner Statistics.* Bureau of Justice Statistics. Washington, DC: U.S. Government Printing Office, 1926– .

This series, published sometimes as individual reports and sometimes as issues of the Bureau of Justice Statistics Bulletin, provides statistics on prisoners in state and federal institutions, prisoners under sentence of death, capital punishment, and jail inmates.

*Sourcebook of Criminal Justice Statistics.* U.S. Department of Justice, Bureau of Justice Statistics. Washington, DC: U.S. Government Printing Office, 1973– . Annual.

This sourcebook is the single, most important compendium of statistics in criminal justice. Note that it is a compilation, a secondary source that presents statistics gathered nationwide from other sources: government agencies, academic institutions, research organizations, and public opinion polling firms. Data cover crime, clearance and arrest rates, personnel and expenditures, courts, probation, persons in correctional institutions, parole, the juvenile justice system, and public opinion. Introduction and appendices offer valuable information, including insight into methodology.

*Uniform Crime Reports (UCR): Crime in the United States.* U.S. Department of Justice, Federal Bureau of Investigation. Washington, DC: U.S. Government Printing Office, 1930– . Annual.

This nationwide view of crime is compiled by the FBI from sixteen thousand reports submitted by city, county, state, and university law enforcement agencies. Be aware that this covers only reported crime and that reporting agencies are not always consistent in the interpretation of issued standards and definitions. UCR's crime index offenses include murders and nonnegligent manslaughter, forcible rape, robbery, aggravated assault, burglary, larceny-theft, motor vehicle theft, and, since 1979, arson. Figures on law enforcement employment are also presented.

## COMPILATIONS OF GENERAL STATISTICS

*Social Indicators III.* U.S. Department of Commerce, Bureau of the Census. Washington, DC: U.S. Government Printing Office, 1980.

Another secondary source utilizing data from other units, this publication contains a section on public safety. Its colorful graphics enhance the presentation of statistics on public perceptions, resource commitments, crime and its victims, public safety indicators, and international comparisons.

*Statistical Abstracts of the United States: National Data Book and Guide to Sources.* U.S. Department of Commerce, Bureau of the Census. Washington, DC: U.S. Government Printing Office, 1878– . Annual.

Under the subject "Law Enforcement, Courts and Prisons" in Appendix IV are listed the sources of statistics reprinted in the section of the book by the same name. Data covers crimes committed, victims of crimes, arrests, prisoners, juvenile offenders, and courts. Easy to use, well indexed, a good ready reference.

## STATE AND LOCAL STATISTICS

Many states publish their own compendiums of statistics. To locate these, look under the geographic name with "Statistics" as a subheading in the library catalog. Local statistics may be found in local government publications, in a municipal reference library, or in the file drawers of a local agency. It may take some good detective work, but persistency usually produces results.

*The Book of the States.* Lexington, KY: The Council of State Governments, 1933– . Biennial.

Statistical tables accompany narrative discussions of trends in state activities. Sources of statistics are noted. Sections on the "Judiciary" and "Safety and Public Protection" yield limited statistics but prove valuable because statistics for all states are collected in a single table.

*Municipal Year Book.* Washington, DC: International City Management Association, 1934– . Annual.

Better known for its overview of current issues in local government and its data on cities and counties, this yearbook also offers detailed statistical tables on police. Figures reveal both personnel and budgetary information. Expenditures as well as salaries are presented for groups of cities, clustered by population size.

## FINDING GUIDES FOR STATISTICAL SOURCES

It is a good idea for the researcher to become acquainted with those organizations and agencies which issue criminal justice statistics. The following items will familiarize you with such sources.

Doleschal, Eugene. "Sources of Basic Criminal Justice Statistics: A Brief Annotated Guide with Commentaries." *Criminal Justice Abstracts* 11:122–147. March, 1979.

This may be dated, but Doleschal does discuss eighteen standard statistical sources in the areas of crime, police, courts, and corrections. Detailed annotations point out the coverage, timeliness, and ease of use for each source.

Parisi, Nicollette. *Sources of National Criminal Justice Statistics: An Annotated Bibliography*. Washington, DC: U.S. Government Printing Office, 1977.

Parisi lists and describes data sources for U.S. statistics. Categories include specialized areas, such as diversions, furloughs, and public opinion, as well as the traditional ones: courts, corrections, crime, drugs, juveniles, and law enforcement. Indexed by subject. Publishers' addresses are noted.

*Statistical Services Directory: A Guide to the Organizations, Corporations, Professional and Trade Associations, Research Centers, Universities, Publishers, Foundations and Government Agencies That Provide Statistical Services*. 2nd ed. Detroit, MI: Gale Research, 1984.

The subtitle says it all. This comprehensive directory details one thousand two hundred primary gatherers and disseminators of statistics. Its detailed subject index ferrets out those units that cover the criminal justice field.

## SELECTED CRIMINAL JUSTICE STATISTICS AGENCIES AND ORGANIZATIONS

American Correctional Association (ACA), 4321 Hartwick Rd., Suite L208, College Park, MD 20740.

ACA's thirteen thousand members study the causes of crime and juvenile delinquency and the methods of crime control and prevention. Individuals under supervision, correctional personnel, parole, recidivism, and financial statistics are included in ACA's annual directory.

Association for Correctional Research and Information Management (ACRIM), c/o Tom Johnson, 600 J St., Division of Criminal Justice, California State University, Sacramento, CA 95819.

Professionals involved in state and federal correctional research and information management systems comprise this association. Its purpose is to provide and improve knowledge, experience, and leadership in the field of correctional research and statistics in such areas as prisons, jails, and juvenile detention centers.

CJAIN: The Criminal Justice Archive and Information Network, P.O. Box 1248, Ann Arbor, MI 48106.

CJAIN is the criminal justice data source located within the Inter-University Consortium for Political and Social Research (ICPSR) at the University of Michigan. ICPSR serves its 275 academic institution members as a central data archive for computer-readable social science data. CJAIN facilitates and encourages research by collecting and disseminating to its members machine-readable data as requested. In addition to Uniform Crime Reports, Bureau of Justice Statistics output and census materials, data tapes, or cards, cover juvenile delinquency, victimization, and the criminal justice system. Ask your professor whether your institution participates in ICPSR and CJAIN. A guide to their resources and services is available.

Criminal Justice Statistics Association (CJSA), 444 N. Capitol Street, NW, Suite 122, Washington, DC 20001.

As liaison between the Federal Bureau of Justice Statistics and the Statistical Analysis Center in each state, CJSA furthers the collection, analyses, dissemination, and use of crime and criminal justice data at the federal and state level. Its members facilitate the identification and transfer of techniques for analyzing criminal justice data.

National Center for Juvenile Justice (NCJJ), 701 Forbes Avenue, Pittsburgh, PA 15219.

Since 1975 NCJJ has collected and disseminated juvenile justice court statistics in order to improve both the quality and quantity of statistics collected. NCJJ is the research division of the National Council of Juvenile and Family Court Judges.

National Center for State Courts (NCSC), 300 Newport Avenue, Williamsburg, VA 23185.

NCSC is composed of representatives from the state courts of the fifty states and five territories. It compiles statistics on state courts' caseloads and administrative operations.

U.S. Administrative Office of the United States Courts, Washington, DC 20544.

Established in 1939, this office, among its other duties, compiles and transmits statistical court data to the Chief Judges of the Circuit Courts, the Attorney General, and the Congress. Reports issued by this office cite statistics on federal judicial workload and on federal offenders in district courts.

U.S. Bureau of the Census, Fourteenth Street between Constitution Avenue and E Street, NW, Washington, DC 20230.

Everyone knows that the Bureau of the Census collects, tabulates, and publishes all sorts of statistical data, while at the same time protecting the confidentiality of the information collected. Its *Detailed Characteristics* and *General Social and Economic Characteristics* present data at the state level, while the *Census Tracts*, *Block Statistics*, and *County and City Data Book* are useful for local data. A valuable spin-off of the census contains information on prison, reformatory, jail, and workhouse populations.

U.S. Federal Bureau of Investigation, Ninth and Pennsylvania Avenue, NW, Washington, DC 20535.

The FBI investigates all violations of federal law except those assigned elsewhere by legislative order. Its most heavily used statistical publication is the *Uniform Crime Report*, but it also issues a bomb summary and reports on assaults on federal officers and on law enforcement officers killed.

U.S. Office of Justice Assistance, Research and Statistics, 633 Indiana Avenue, NW, Washington, DC 20531.

This umbrella unit coordinates the activities and provides staff support to the Bureau of Justice Statistics, the National Institute of Justice, and the Office of Juvenile Justice and Delinquency Prevention.

U.S. Bureau of Justice Statistics (BJS), 633 Indiana Avenue, NW, Washington, DC 20531.

Within the Department of Justice and its office listed above one would expect to find a major division for the collection and dispersal of statistical reports. The Bureau of Justice Statistics serves just that purpose. For all levels of government it collects, analyzes, publishes, and disseminates statistical information on crime, victims of crime, criminal offenders, and operations of the criminal justice system. State statistical agencies receive financial and technical support from this bureau, as well as policy guidance on exchange of criminal records and data privacy, confidentiality, and security. Its *Bureau of Justice Statistics Bulletin* makes available statistical information on parole and probation, state and federal courts, justice expenditures and employment privacy and security, white-collar crime, computer crime, and on other topics of concern for criminal justice research. BJS materials are indexed in the *Monthly Catalog*, in *American Statistics Index*, and in *Document Retrieval Index*. Its data tapes are available through CJAIN.

## STATISTICS AND PUBLIC OPINION POLLS

Public opinion on specific issues is determined by interviewing a segment of the population. Elaborate sampling procedures have been developed over the years to produce poll results that eliminate bias and more accurately reflect actual public views. Sophisticated computer methodology has enhanced polling techniques. First developed as private business enterprises, public opinion polls have moved onto university campuses and into the offices of leading newspapers and television companies. Concerned with politics, government, social conditions, economic policy, and foreign issues, pollsters often turn the spotlight on crime and the justice system. Such statistical reflections of public opinion can prove useful to your research. Surveys have been conducted on such topics as sentencing, the fear of crime, gun control, capital punishment, the public level of confidence in the police and the courts, law enforcement, legalization of marijuana, and victimization. Poll results are broadcast on radio and television and printed in newspapers, periodicals, and special publications.

### Guides to Public Opinion Poll Results

*American Public Opinion Index*. Louisville, KY: Opinion Research Service, 1981– . Annual.

This yearly survey describes polls conducted in America. Entries are under the subject of the survey and note its source. Section II states the full address of the unit conducting the survey, the date, sample size, method, universe, and special topic. A microfiche set, *American Public Opinion Data*, accompanies the index.

*Index to International Public Opinion*.

See entry in chapter XIV.

*Newspaper and Magazine Indexes and Abstracts.*

Printed results of polls frequently appear first in newspapers and periodicals. Thus they are indexed along with the other articles in newspaper and periodical indexes. Most such indexes will use "Public Opinion" or "Public Opinion Polls" as a subject heading. They will also use the term as a subheading under the topic of the poll. For instance, if you are looking for the results of a survey on capital punishment you may find it under "Capital Punishment—Public Opinion." Because public opinion polls are attuned to current social issues, their topics often suggest possibilities for research. A good source for locating hot topics.

## Major Sources for Public Opinion Polls

The ABC/Washington Post Poll, ABC News Polling Unit, 7 West 66 St., New York, NY 10023.

CBS News/New York Times Poll, CBS News, 524 W. 57th St., New York, NY 10019.

NBC News/Associated Press Poll, National Broadcasting Company, 30 Rockefeller Plaza. New York, NY 10020.

In general, newspapers and broadcasting companies extract public opinion through telephone interviews across the country. Samples of telephone exchanges are matched with random digits in such a way that both listed and unlisted numbers have a properly proportionate chance to be called. Results of these polls are printed not only in the sponsoring papers but also in magazines and other periodicals. Criminal justice topics appear in the polls with surprising regularity.

American Association for Public Opinion Research, P.O. Box 17, Princeton, NJ 08542.

Individuals, agencies, and organizations join this association to share their interests in the methodology and applications of social and public opinion research. It publishes *Public Opinion Quarterly*.

*Public Opinion Quarterly*. New York: Elsevier Science Publishing, 1937– . Quarterly.

This scholarly journal presents articles on polling methodology and on specific polls and poll results from various survey organizations. It is the most heavily indexed of the polling journals, appearing in *Current Contents*, *Public Affairs Information Service Bulletin*, *Psychological Abstracts*, *Social Science Citation Index*, and *Social Sciences Index*.

American Enterprise Institute for Public Policy Research, 1150 Seventeenth Street, NW, Washington, DC 20036.

Since 1943 the stated aim of this institute has been "to assist policy makers, scholars, businessmen, the press and the public by providing objective analyses of national and international issues." To this end it carries on an active publishing program, including *Public Opinion*.

*Public Opinion*. Washington, DC: American Enterprise Institute for Public Policy Research, 1978– . Bimonthly.

A feature of *Public Opinion* is "Opinion Roundup," which reprints data on a variety of topics from several public opinion survey sources. Polls are graphically presented in color. *Public Opinion* is indexed in *Social Sciences Index*.

The Gallup Report, P.O. Box 628, Princeton, NJ 08542.

George Gallup founded the American Institute of Public Opinion in 1935. Since then his name has been a household word because of his interest in survey research, public opinion, and politics. Rare indeed is the person who has not heard of the Gallup Poll. His cumulated volumes (1935–1971 and 1972–1977) and the annual volumes since then include indexes. Use these indexes to find survey results on criminal justice subjects. Results of Gallup Polls are published in newspapers and periodicals and also monthly in the following journal:

*The Gallup Report*. (Formerly *The Gallup Opinion Index* and *The Gallup Political Index*.) Princeton, NJ: The Gallup Poll, 1965– . Monthly.

Indexed in *Public Affairs Information Service*.

Louis Harris and Associates, 630 5th Avenue, New York, NY 10020.

Louis Harris Data Center, Chapel Hill, NC 27514.

Since 1956 Louis Harris and Associates has conducted surveys. It releases *The Harris Survey* twice weekly. Results of this group's questioning appear in newspapers across the country. In 1966 the Louis Harris Data Center was established at Chapel Hill, North Carolina, as an integral part of the Institute for Research in the Social Sciences. This center serves as a data storage and retrieval facility for research in the social sciences.

The National Opinion Research Center (NORC), 6030 South Ellis Avenue, Chicago, IL 60637.

Affiliated with the University of Chicago, the nonprofit NORC began in 1941 as the first noncommercial opinion research agency in the country. Supported by grants and contracts, results of its research are published in professional journals, project reports, and monographs. Its concern with policy studies and problems of urbanization are of interest to those in the criminal justice field.

Roper Center for Public Opinion Research, U-164R, University of Connecticut, Storrs, CT 06268.

The Roper Center is affiliated with the University of Connecticut, Yale University, and Williams College. Nonprofit, it is supported by its parent institutions, industry, and subscribers. The Roper Center provides data to public opinion researchers and the public policy community. It concerns itself with public affairs, public policy, and political behavior and attitudes. Results of Roper's surveys appear in newspapers, magazines, books, and in the center-published *Public Opinion*.

*Public Opinion*. (Formerly *Current Opinion*.) Storrs, CT: Roper Center for Public Opinion Research, 1973– . Monthly.

This journal presents poll results of surveys by leading public opinion groups. Criminal justice topics are included.

# XI

# Printed Bibliographies and Guides to the Literature

Compiling a bibliography is like rolling a snowball downhill—it picks up size and momentum en route. One of the most efficient ways to add to the list of titles you are collecting for your research is to locate a useful bibliography. In truth, finding a good bibliography is like having someone else do your work for you.

## PRINTED BIBLIOGRAPHIES

### Kinds of Bibliographies

Bibliographies are as varied as the persons who use them. They can be short, long, selective, comprehensive, simple, or complex. They can be arranged alphabetically, by author or title, or clustered under certain topics. Bibliographies may pull together items on a specific subject, by a single author, in a specified format, or in a special collection. They may vary in length from a simple list of a few items to a multivolume set of bound volumes. They may cite only current items; only older items, in which case they are called retrospective bibliographies; or a combination of both. By definition, bibliographies are lists of works, parts of works, or documents with a common factor among them.

### When to Use Printed Bibliographies

Bibliographies often provide an overview of a discipline because representative works of subject authorities in the field are selected for inclusion. In a certain sense bibliographies are analogous to encyclopedias in the information flow. While encyclopedias offer synthesis and analysis of the content of a subject, bibliographies offer synthesis and analysis of items available in the literature of a particular subject. As such, bibliographies can save the researcher hours of time. The more related the subject matter of a bibliography is to the topic under investigation, the more valuable it becomes to the researcher.

The researcher must decide the role bibliographies should play in any particular project. If the paper is short, if the library has an abundance of material on the subject, if indexes provide more than adequate coverage, there is really little advantage to seeking out bibliographies. When the research should be exhaustive, when very little information is readily available, when there is adequate time to utilize interlibrary loan, bibliographies will greatly enhance the research.

### How to Find Bibliographies

It is often true that libraries with inadequate collections in a particular subject will purposely collect bibliographies in that subject area. Such bibliographies then provide users with access to titles and possibly to sources for obtaining these titles through interlibrary loan. That is why all research libraries and many academic libraries purchase extensive numbers of bibliographies. As you work in your library and with your librarian you will soon discover the role bibliographies can play in your research.

Locating bibliographies is not difficult. Bibliographies are listed in guides and found at the ends of books, articles, documents, and dissertations. There are even bibliographies that list other bibliographies. If you find an item that is valuable for your research, chances are that many items in its bibliography will be equally useful.

Book-length bibliographies appear in library catalogs as the subdivision –Bibliography under specific subjects. It is a subdivision which can be used with any subject. Try Ex-convicts–Bibliography; Criminal justice, administration of–Bibliography; or Police wives–Bibliography.

Computer literature searches always result in custom-made bibliographies. Keep them in mind.

### How to Use Bibliographies

Use bibliographies skillfully. Check the publication date and introduction to determine coverage. Do not, however, be misled by the publication date of a bibliography. Rather check the dates the compiler tells you it covers, or scan the entries to find the earliest and latest dates there. Be wary of those listing only the first edition of a series with no indication whether it is still being published. Read critically whatever annotations are available. Conceivably, a bibliography could reflect the compiler's bias. It goes without saying that you will evaluate entries from someone's bibliography before transferring them to your own.

Be reminded again: if your need is high and resources are low, use bibliographies to find titles you can borrow through interlibrary loan. This procedure may prove to be your best resource.

## BIBLIOGRAPHIES OF BIBLIOGRAPHIES

These are valuable bibliographies that list only other bibliographies.

### Criminal Justice

Davis, Bruce L. *Criminological Bibliographies: Uniform Citations to Bibliographies, Indexes, and Review Articles of the Literature of Crime Study in the United States*. Westport, CT: Greenwood Press, 1978.

Detailed subject indexes precede each of the seven subdivisions covering the administration and social aspects of criminal justice. Over one thousand four hundred bibliographies, indexes, catalogs, and review articles, uniformly cited, chronicle America's criminal justice bibliographic literature. Since many entries go back to the nineteenth century, this list is useful for historical studies. Selected locations where listed items may be found are noted. A benchmark publication.

Klein, Carol, and David M. Horton, comps. *Bibliographies in Criminal Justice: A Selected Bibliography*. Washington, DC: U.S. Department of Justice, National Criminal Justice Reference Service, 1979.

Reflected in this listing are 222 bibliographies including not only those produced by NCJRS staff but also those held by the NCJRS library. Descriptive annotations prove long enough to reflect accurately the contents of the cited titles.

Marcus, Marvin. *Criminal Justice Bibliography*. 2nd ed. Atlanta, GA: Georgia State University, School of Urban Life, 1976.

Lists over 6,000 bibliographies under 184 categories. Author, subject indexes. Some very brief annotations. Extensive coverage offsets its difficult-to-read, early generation computer format.

Ross, John M. *National Criminal Justice Reference Services (NCJRS) Bibliographies: A Bibliography of Bibliographies*. CPL Bibliography No. 103. Chicago: CPL Bibliographies, 1983.

This publication collects in a single source a list of the bibliographies prepared by the NCJRS staff. Brief annotations reveal the scope of each citation and give its NCJ and SuDocs call numbers. Locate the cited bibliographies in the government documents collection of your library or in the NCJRS microfiche collection. While this duplicates in part *Bibliographies in Criminal Justice*, its later publication date allows inclusion of additional titles published through 1982.

### General

*Bibliographic Index*. New York: H. W. Wilson, 1938– . Quarterly.

Easy to use, this is an alphabetical subject and author index to bibliographies of fifty or more entries. The bibliography indexed might be published separately or as part of a book, pamphlet, or article. The index is cumulated quarterly and annually. General in scope, it contains such criminal justice entries as "rape victims," "victims of crime," "criminal courts," and "rehabilitation of criminals." Check also under other standard criminal justice topics.

Kanely, Edna A., comp. *Cumulative Subject Guide to U.S. Government Bibliographies, 1924–1973*. 7 vols. Arlington, VA: Carrollton Press, 1976.

An ambitious undertaking, this multivolume set extracts from the *Monthly Catalog* forty thousand bibliographies published separately or within other federal documents issued between 1924 and 1973. Considering the government's omniscience, you should find useful titles under your specific subject. Entries fortunately include SuDocs call numbers, with the final volume indexing the entries under these call numbers.

## SELECTED USEFUL BIBLIOGRAPHIES

*A Bibliography of Selected Rand Publications*. Santa Monica, CA: Rand, 1984.

The Rand Corporation públishes a series of bibliographies noting items it has issued in the areas of *Criminal Justice*, *Civil Justice*, and *Public Safety*. Annotated entries describe the books, reports, notes, memoranda, and papers of this well-known think tank.

Cordasco, Francesco, and David Nelson Alloway. *Crime in America: Historical Patterns and Contemporary Realities*. New York: Garland, 1985.

Concentrating on items published since 1975, the authors briefly annotate almost two thousand references to books, journal articles, reports, and documents. Includes practitioner-slanted entries, covering general topics, basic sources, periodicals, and organizations.

*Crime and Punishment in America: A Historical Bibliography*. Santa Barbara, CA: ABC-Clio Information Services, 1984.

Compendium of 1,396 abstracts of articles on the history of crime in America published during 1973–1982. In-depth indexing offers multipoint access, a boon to the researcher.

Doleschal, Eugene, Anne Newton, and William Hickey. *A Guide to the Literature on Organized Crime: An Annotated Bibliography Covering the Years 1967–1981*. Hackensack, NJ: National Council on Crime and Delinquency, 1981.

The title tells it all. Be aware that this bibliography documents the major change in scholarly thought on the origins, nature, and control of organized crime, particularly since publication of the President's Commission on Law Enforcement and Administration of Justice *Task Force Report*.

Jerath, Bal K., Paul E. Larson, and Jesse F. Lewis. *Homicide: A Bibliography of Over 4,500 Items*. Augusta, GA: Pine Tree Publications, 1982.

An extensive subject index adds to this classified listing of homicide ecology and epidemiology.

Regoli, Robert M., John D. Hewitt, and Eric D. Poole. *Criminal Justice in America, 1960–1984: An Annotated Bibliography*. NY: Garland, 1985.

Under each of three main types—Law enforcement, Courts, and Corrections—the authors have subdivided entries by history, organization, process, and issues. Its almost one thousand entries are indexed by personal name and subject.

Vom Ende, Rudolf. *Criminology and Forensic Sciences: An International Bibliography, 1950–1980*. 3 vols. Munich: Saur, 1981.

An alphabetical author index to journal and monographic materials. No subject index. Useful if you are checking the works of a specific writer.

Whitehouse, Jack. *Police Bibliography*. New York: AMS Press, 1980.

17,400 book and article entries cover the wide spectrum of police activity.

Wilson, Carolyn F. *Violence against Women: An Annotated Bibliography*. Boston: G. K. Hall, 1981.

Author Wilson concentrates on journal articles appearing from 1975 to 1980. Entries are annotated and indexed by author/title and subject.

## SELECTED OLDER BIBLIOGRAPHIES

Beyleveld, Deryck. *The Effectiveness of General Deterrents against Crime: An Annotated Bibliography of Evaluative Research*. Cambridge: University of Cambridge Institute of Criminology, 1978.

An unusually thorough bibliography on this topic. Annotations are quite detailed and a good system of cross-references make this source a very productive one.

*Economics of Crime and Correction*. Washington, DC: American Bar Association, Correctional Economics Center, 1974.

This brief bibliography pulls together material on meeting the challenge of fiscal responsibility and on planning based on sound fiscal principles. An example of a specialized bibliography dealing with a specific aspect of criminal justice.

Felkenes, George T., and Harold K. Becker. *Law Enforcement: A Selected Bibliography*. 2nd ed. Metuchen, NJ: Scarecrow Press, 1977.

The emphasis in this bibliography is on the interdisciplinary nature of criminal justice as revealed in journal literature.

Johnson, Emily, and Marjorie Kravitz, comps. *Basic Sources in Criminal Justice: A Selected Bibliography*. Washington, DC: U.S. National Criminal Justice Reference Service, 1978.

General in scope, listing only 259 items, this bibliography contains extensive discussions of each item. Particularly helpful are descriptions of individual commission reports.

Goehlert, Robert. *Research Resources in Criminology*. Public Administration Series Bibliography P-245. Monticello, IL: Vance Bibliographies, 1979.

Classified arrangement includes federal publications and federal statistical sources. One of a public administration bibliography series that often includes criminal justice issues. Check the series for other titles.

Mersky, Roy M., Robert C. Berring, and James K. McCue. *Authors Guide to Journals in Law, Criminal Justice and Criminology*. New York: Haworth, 1979.

Note that this source profiles only periodicals in the field. A good one-step source to locate detailed information as well as learn the journal titles in the field. Indexed.

Prostano, Emmanuel. *Law Enforcement*. Littleton, CO: Libraries Unlimited, 1974.

This subject arrangement with author and title indexes covers information published between 1967 and 1972. Includes audiovisual material.

Simpson, Antony E., and Nina Duchaine. *The Literature of Police Corruption*. 2 vols. New York: John Jay, 1977–79.

Both a review of the literature and a bibliography of six hundred titles comprise volume 1. Dissertations and textbooks are included in the four hundred titles noted in volume 2.

Suvak, Daniel. *Memoirs of American Prisons*. Metuchen, NJ: Scarecrow, 1979.

Annotated entries reveal experiences of civil, voluntary, and military prisoners. Indexed by name, title, and prison name.

Triche, Charles W., III. *The Capital Punishment Dilemma, 1950–1977: A Subject Bibliography*. Troy, NY: Whitson, 1979.

Lists books and essays and indexes periodical literature under broad subjects. Some foreign-language entries.

von Pfeil, Helena P. *Juvenile Rights Since 1967*. Littleton, CO: Rothman, 1974.

Books and articles are arranged under author's name, indexed by subject. Some annotations.

## CLASSICS IN THE FIELD

### Criminal Justice

Culver, Dorothy Campbell. *Bibliography of Crime and Criminal Justice, 1927–1931*. 1934. Reprint. Montclair, NJ: Patterson Smith, 1969.

———. *Bibliography of Crime and Criminal Justice, 1932–1937*. 1939. Reprint. Montclair, NJ: Patterson Smith, 1969.

Tompkins, Dorothy Campbell Culver. *Sources for the Study of the Administration of Criminal Justice, 1938–1948: A Selected Bibliography*. 1949. Reprint. Montclair, NJ: Patterson Smith, 1970.

———. *Administration of Criminal Justice, 1949–1956*. 1956. Reprint. Montclair, NJ: Patterson Smith, 1970.

This series of classified bibliographies emanated from Berkeley's Bureau of Public Administration (now the Institute of Governmental Studies). Coverage is comprehensive for books and journals, including some foreign language. All are indexed. Follow-up bibliographies were done by the author: *The Offender* (1963), *Probation Since World War II* (1964), *White Collar Crime* (1967), *Sentencing the Offender* (1971), and *The Prison and the Prisoner* (1971).

Cuming, Sir John. *Contribution towards a Bibliography Dealing with Crime and Cognate Subjects*. 3rd ed. 1935. Reprint. Montclair, NJ: Patterson Smith, 1970.

British-classified list covering fifty years. International in scope. Considered the basic nineteenth- and early twentieth-century police bibliography. Author and combined subject and geographical indexes.

Klein, Fannie J. *Administration of Justice in the Courts*. 2 vols. Dobbs Ferry, NY: Oceana Publications, 1976.

Two-volume coverage of books and journals through early 1975 dealing with courts and criminal justice in the courts. Annotations note distinctive features of titles. Entries also by state. Indexes include name, subject, and table of cases.

Kuhlman, Augustus F. *Guide to Material on Crime and Criminal Justice*. 1929. Reprint. Montclair, NJ: Patterson Smith, 1969.

An author index was added to this comprehensive reprint list of books, pamphlets, and articles in a classified arrangement. Covers American and British materials published before 1927. The subject index is at the front of the volume.

Radzinowicz, Leon, and Roger Hood. *Criminology and the Administration of Criminal Justice: A Bibliography*. Westport, CT: Greenwood Press, 1976.

Authors carefully selected and evaluated contemporary books, articles, and reports through August 1974, then bound-in a lengthy supplement to update selections to February 1976. Annotations are brief. Entries are classified and arranged in each class from earliest to most recent. Focus is sociological with an emphasis on policy.

Rank, Richard. *The Criminal Justice Systems of the Latin-American Nations: A Bibliography of the Primary and Secondary Literatures*. South Hackensack, NJ: Fred B. Rothman, 1974.

Over nine thousand entries are arranged in classified order under individual areas including Central and South America, Cuba, the Dominican Republic, Haiti, and Puerto Rico.

Wolfgang, Marvin E., Robert M. Figlio, and Terence P. Thornberry. *Criminology Index*. 2 vols. New York: Elsevier Science Publishing, 1975.

This two-volume citation index covers periodical literature from 1945 to 1972. It is a challenge to use because of its arrangement but includes valuable citations.

## General

*International Bibliography of the Social Sciences: International Bibliography of Sociology*. London: Tavistock; Chicago: Aldine, 1952– . Annual.

Multilanguage classified listing of books, pamphlets, articles, and official publications. Scholarly selective.

*London Bibliography of the Social Sciences*. London: London School of Economics, 1931– . Five-year and annual supplements.

Subject approach to international resources, with good coverage of legislative, administrative, and official reports.

## GUIDES TO THE LITERATURE

Rather than list and give a brief summary of an entry, guides tend to compare, contrast, evaluate, or explain the usage of material noted.

*Criminal Justice Abstracts*. (Formerly *Abstracts on Crime and Delinquency, Crime and Delinquency Literature*.) Monsey, NY: Willow Tree, 1968– . Quarterly.

Be reminded that the issues of this publication contain reviews of the literature on specific topics of concern.

O'Block, Robert L. *Criminal Justice Research Sources*. Cincinnati, OH: Anderson, 1983.

Fashioned to lead students to available materials, this guide lists or annotates sources and recommends procedures for conducting research in criminal justice. Appendices 1 and 2 are especially clear introductions to research steps and to writing a term paper.

Williams, Vergil Lewis. "Administration of Criminal Justice: A Bibliographical Selection." *Choice* 9 (July–August 1972): 611–618.

Williams notes the six functions of criminal justice as police, prosecutors, courts, probation, corrections, and parole, presenting a fine review of the noteworthy literature of the 1960's and early 1970's. About twenty items predate that period. Would that the criminal justice literature of other time periods were reviewed as effectively.

Wright, Martin, ed. *Use of Criminology Literature*. Hamden, CT: Shoe String, 1974.

Contributors discuss the major literature of the United Kingdom and the United States devoted to various aspects of criminology. Valuable contrasts and comparisons are made, mainly of twentieth-century materials.

# Part 3

# SOME SPECIAL PROBLEMS

# XII

# Research in Legal Resources

The purpose of this chapter is not to teach legal research as the term is used by lawyers; rather it is to help criminal justice researchers exploit legal resources to buttress and enrich studies in their own field.

After mastering the material in this chapter you should be able to use legal resources to do the following:

1. Find a citation if you know only the name or popular name of a case, statute, or regulation;
2. Locate the latest additions to the law;
3. Locate all the cases or current law in force on a particular topic;
4. Determine if what you have found is still valid or "good law";
5. Locate discussions of general legal topics;
6. Locate discussions of specific laws, cases, and regulations.

## GAINING ACCESS TO LAW BOOKS

Legal resources are more widely available than many people think. If your library does not have the material you need, ask your librarian for advice on where to go, or contact the nearest federal, state, or county courthouse. Often the lawyers who use court system libraries (and the librarians who run them) view the resources as their exclusive property. In many cases, however, these libraries, because they are supported by public funds, are indeed open to the public. You may find access to libraries in law schools more difficult to achieve, but many of them do permit outsiders to use their resources. A letter of introduction or a telephone call from your own librarian may help.

First encounters with law libraries are frequently intimidating even to experienced library users. The books are overwhelming in number and appearance, the librarian, although knowledgeable, may not be accustomed to helping those who are just learning to use legal materials, and the other patrons somehow all look as if they know exactly what they are doing.

*Hint:* Before going to a law library, read this chapter carefully, get as much help as you can from your own librarian, and, if possible, consult one of the legal research guides listed at the end of this chapter. When you get to the law library remember: don't be intimidated by either the people or the books.

## THE AMERICAN LEGAL SYSTEM AND ITS PUBLICATIONS

American law has four basic components, each of which exists on the federal and state levels:

1. The Constitution;
2. Statute Law—the statutes, or laws, passed by the legislatures;
3. Regulatory Law—rules and regulations promulgated by government agencies that have the force of law;
4. Case Law—the interpretations of the other three made by the courts as a result of cases brought to them on appeal.

The law is a living entity with statutes, regulations, and case law constantly being nullified, added to, and revised. Understanding the manner in which these changes and additions progress through the various types of legal publications—the information flow—will enable you to plot the research strategy that will best serve your needs.

Legal resources are often a pleasant surprise for the first-time user. They follow a logical and thoroughly consistent pattern of publication. Once that pattern is understood it is relatively simple to decide the proper source to consult to solve your problem.

Because it is essential for lawyers, politicians, and the public to have access to the most current additions and changes, all new and revised elements of the law appear fairly quickly in published form. The first appearance is chronological with the publication arranged simply by the date of the decision or ruling. Such chronological publications, however, do not cumulate and would be very difficult to use to locate all the law on a particular topic. Thus, there are frequent republications of the law in subject format.

## STRATEGIES FOR THE USE OF LEGAL RESOURCES

### Before Starting

Your work will be easier if you can decide before starting whether your research involves federal or state sources; whether it involves statute, regulatory, or case law; and what level of information is needed—historical precedent, law currently in force, or only the most recent revisions or additions.

### Reading Legal Citations

Although they look as if they were designed to bedevil the unwary, legal citations are actually simple to decipher. A legal citation is just a standardized way of referring to a specific element in the law. It has three basic parts: a volume number, an abbreviation for the title, and a page or section number. These are sometimes followed by the date.

The following are examples of legal citations:

Supreme Court Case: 383 US 463 (1966). This means volume 383 of the *United States Reports*, page 463, decided in 1966.

Federal Law: 42 USC §1971 (1976). This means title 42 of the *United States Code*, section 1971, passed in 1976.

Federal Regulation: 28 CFR 42.6. This means title 28 of the *Code of Federal Regulations*, section 42.6

Journal: 131 U.Pa.L.Rev 353–387, Dec '82. This means volume 131 of the University of Pennsylvania Law Review, pages 353 to 387, from December 1982.

### Using the Indexes in Law Books

There are significant differences between the index of a law book and that of other books. Law books tend to use broad rather than narrow terms as index entries, with the narrower concepts used only as subdivisions of the more encompassing word.

It is helpful to begin your search by compiling a list of all possible synonyms, broader terms, and narrower terms that apply to your topic. Expect to check most of them before finding exactly what is needed. Although this may be surprisingly time consuming, in the end it will save you from wasting time reading material that is not relevant.

### Exploring Tables of Contents

Most legal publications that have a subject arrangement, such as encyclopedias, digests, and codified arrangements of statutes and regulations, have very detailed tables of contents before each section or article. In some cases there will be a general table of contents followed by one or more increasingly detailed analytical tables of contents. It is not unusual for these tables to be over ten pages. Don't rush through them; they give an overview of the entire topic and can help isolate the specific paragraph which will help to answer your question. In general, time spent reading an analytical table of contents is time not wasted reading material irrelevant to your research.

### Updating with Pocket Parts

Lawyers need to have the most up-to-date information. Chronological publications are automatically updated each time a new volume is issued. Publications that are arranged by subject are more difficult to keep up-to-date. Legal publishers, however, make use of a unique device for keeping their alphabetically arranged publications current. Called a *pocket part*, it is a separate part, or pamphlet, that is inserted into a pocket in the back cover of the volume that it updates. Never consider that you have finished using a legal publication until you have consulted the pocket part to see whether or not the information you have just read is still valid. Lawyers generally look at the pocket part first. Remember: index volumes also have pocket parts.

### Computerized Access to the Law

There are two major systems that provide online access to the basic components of the law. *WESTLAW*, a product of the West Publishing Company, and *LEXIS*, produced by Mead Data Central, are both complex systems, providing a variety of search options and both full-text and indexing outputs. Both can only be accessed through a separate subscription, are quite expensive, and are unlikely to be available any place other than a law library, court system, or large law firm.

Some publications of interest to researchers in this area may be accessed online through the more generally available services. These have been indicated in the annotations.

## STATUTE LAW

Statute law is that body of law which is passed by a legislative unit.

### Federal Statutes

At the federal level a bill becomes a law after it is passed by both houses of the legislature and is signed by the president.

### *Chronological Publication*

*Slip Law*. Washington, DC: U.S. Government Printing Office.

*U.S. Code Congressional and Administrative News Service*. St. Paul, MN: West, 1939– .

*Advance Sheets, United States Code Service, Lawyers' Edition*. New York: Lawyers' Co-op; San Francisco: Bancroft-Whitney, 1972– .

After passage, laws are sent to the Administrator of General Services and designated a public or private law. Private laws benefit only specific individuals and are seldom of concern for your research. Laws are given two-part numbers, the first part indicating the number of Congress, the second its sequential place. PL 96–210 would be the 210th law passed by the 96th Congress. Laws are printed first by the U.S. Government Printing Office as *slip laws*. The slip law is identified by its public law number and its Statutes at Large citation. Following the text of the law is its legislative history, including House and Senate Reports, conference reports, *Congressional Record* notations, and presidential statements that appear in the *Weekly Compilation of Presidential Documents*. Slip laws are also reproduced in full text in the commercial sources above.

*U.S. Statutes at Large*. Boston: Little, Brown, 1789–1873; Washington, DC: U.S. Government Printing Office, 1875– .

At the end of a Congressional session slip laws are reprinted in numerical order in *U.S. Statutes at Large*. Each volume of *Statutes* is indexed by subject and contains a table listing how each public law in this volume affects any previous public law. Remember that these sources publish the law in chronological order.

### *Subject Publication*

The next published format of the U.S. law is the *Code*. This codification process brings together the laws on a subject, unites the original law with all changes, and eliminates repealed, superseded, or expired laws.

*United States Code*. Washington, DC: U.S. Government Printing Office, 1926– .

The first official *U.S. Code* was not published until 1926 when all repealed sections of the *Revised Statutes of 1875* and all subsequent volumes of *Statutes at Large* were arranged into a single set of fifty titles. This official version of the *Code* is reissued every six years by the U.S. Government Printing Office. Bound cumulative supplements accommodate the years between each revision. Available online: *LEXIS*.

*United States Code Annotated* (*USCA*). St. Paul, MN: West, 1927– .

*United States Code Service, Lawyers' Edition* (*USCS*). Rochester, NY: Lawyers' Co-op, 1972– .

Because the meaning of a law is not always clear, its interpretation frequently is clarified by court decisions. Annotated codes, published by commercial firms, include brief summaries of such cases. These annotated codes provide more detailed indexing than the official one; are more current because they are updated by pocket pages, pamphlets, and replacement volumes; and are enriched by federal and state court decisions plus citations to the *Code of Federal Regulations*, Attorney Generals' opinions, and historical notes. Easier to use, the annotated versions give the researcher access to not only the law but supplementary information vital to its interpretation. *USCA* is available online: *WESTLAW*.

### Locating Acts by Popular Name

Often statutes are known by popular names, usually based on the subject of the act or its authors. The Omnibus Crime Control and Safe Streets Act does not reveal to researchers its year of passage, its public law number, or the title where it is encoded. Neither does an act title based on authors' names, such as the Stevenson-Wydler Technology Innovation Act. All versions of the *Code* contain indexes to acts by their popular names. In the official *Code*'s "General Index" is an "Index of Acts by Popular Names." *USCA*, in both its index volume and many title volume indexes, includes tables of acts by popular names. *USCS* has a "Table of Acts by Popular Names" in its table volumes.

A separate publication is:

*Shepard's Acts and Cases by Popular Names, Federal and State*. 2d ed. Colorado Springs, CO: Shepard's, 1979– .

Here acts are listed alphabetically by name with the citation given to locate the source. You will need to use the appropriate *Statutes at Large* for the public law version or an edition of the *Code* to locate the codified version.

### Finding the Current Law

To locate current law in force in the official version of the *Code*, the latest edition, plus each supplement, must be consulted. To utilize the annotated versions, consult the latest edition, its pocket parts, or any supplemental pamphlet. Look first in the general index under the topic. Remember the indexes in the annotated versions are more detailed. Next use the indexes in the individual titles. These will lead to appropriate sections within the titles. Remember the most current codified law—if changes have been made—will be found in the official supplements and the pocket parts and pamphlets.

### Tracking Current Legislation

Current legislation receives exhaustive coverage in easy-to-find and easy-to-use sources.

*Congressional Index*. Chicago: Commerce Clearing House, 1953/54– .

A loose-leaf service, its weekly updates index legislation for each Congress by subject, author, and bill number. It includes summaries, the progress and status of bills, and voting records.

*Congressional Quarterly Weekly Report*. Washington, DC: Congressional Quarterly, 1971– . Weekly.

This journal features articles about legislation, revealing its intent by providing background material. It includes summaries of bills and voting records on the bills and of the legislators.

*Congressional Record* (*CR*) Washington, DC: U.S. Government Printing Office, 1873/74– . Daily.

The official record of Congress, published daily during sessions, its fortnightly index includes an "Index to Proceedings" and a "History of Bills and Resolutions." Access is by subject, sponsor, and bill number. The final bound issue at the end of a session includes a comprehensive status table for bills enacted into law. *CR* is available online through *Dialog* and *SDC*.

*Major Legislation of the Congress*. Washington, DC: U.S. Government Printing Office, 1980– . Monthly.

Published during the sessions of Congress, this resource summarizes Congressional issues and whatever major legislation is introduced in response to those issues. At the end of each Congress a cumulative summary issue is distributed.

### *Legislative Histories*

The legislative history of a law is a record of the documents considered by a legislature during the course of deliberations. Legislative histories are consulted to help understand the reasons for enactment, to aid in interpreting the intent of a law, to discover background information, and to shed light on the social and political environment of the deliberations.

Legislative histories of a public law gather together the various forms of a Congressional bill, its committee reports, Congressional debates, committee hearings, and supporting documents.

The most valuable access to legislative histories from 1970 to the present is the Abstract volume of *CIS/Index*.

*CIS/Index*. Washington, DC: Congressional Information Service, 1970– .

Legislative histories, formerly comprising a section within *CIS/Abstracts* and since 1984 compiled in a separate volume, are arranged by public law numbers of the Congress covered. In addition to the bill, the hearings, and committee prints, the entries also note references appearing in the *Weekly Compilation of Presidential Documents*. Remember that many libraries own the microfiche collection of *CIS*-indexed documents, giving you immediate access to the documents comprising the legislative history. This is the quickest and most efficient source for legislative histories since 1970.

Johnson, Nancy P. *Sources of Compiled Legislative Histories*. Littleton, CO: Rothman, 1981.

A guide to sources for the study of legislative history, this resource includes government documents, periodical articles, or books. Does not include all public laws enacted but covers significant laws passed by the 1st through 94th Congresses. Loose-leaf format.

*Major Studies of the Legislative Reference Service/Congressional Research Service* (*CRS*). Arlington, VA: University Publications of America, 1975– .

This microfilm collection, with supplements, includes Congressional Reference Service studies of major legislation from 1916 on. *CRS* is the research resource for members of Congress.

*Public Laws—Legislative Histories; Microfiche*. Chicago: Commerce Clearing House, 1979– .

Available on microfiche are the bills as introduced in the House or Senate, the reported bill, committee reports, conference reports, if any, and pertinent debates as reported in the *Congressional Record*. Indexes are by subject, public law number, and bill number.

Legislative histories for earlier bills may be compiled by consulting appropriate editions of the *Congressional Index* and the *Congressional Record*. Inexperienced searchers, at this point, should seek aid from the librarian.

## State Statutes

State laws follow the same general pattern of organization and publication as federal laws. Laws will be passed by the legislature, published in chronological order, then incorporated into a code. Often the chronological order carries the title "session laws." The code will usually have "revised," "compiled," or "consolidated" in its title. Most volumes of state law will include the state's constitution, its laws arranged by subject, historical notes, annotations, and tables. For some states published guides, often written by law librarians, contain the legal history and organization of the state government. Such resources will clarify areas of confusion and lead you to useful research resources. Check with your librarian. If a guide is available, it will save you time and effort.

At present no single manual or computerized source exists to provide a comprehensive index to statutes of all states. Be forewarned: comparative research in state law will prove time consuming.

### *Useful Resources*

*Criminal Justice Statutory Index*. Lexington, KY: Council of State Governments, 1975.

By states, this volume describes legislative statutes dealing with such topics as gun control, victimless crimes, judicial selection and review, and capital punishment. Cites pertinent sections of state codes. Issued in 1980 on microfiche.

Nyberg, Cheryl, and Carol Boast. *Subject Compilation of State Laws: Research Guide and Annotated Bibliography*. 2d ed. Westport, CT: Greenwood Press, 1984.

The complexities of research in state laws is effectively explored in the guide section of this excellent aid. Its bibliography section facilitates comparative studies of state laws by listing citations under subjects such as prosecution, sentencing, bribery, and capital punishment. Supplements 1981 edition by Lynn Foster and Carol Boast.

*Martindale Hubbell Law Directory*. New York: Martindale Hubbell, 1931– . Annual.

Its "Law Digest" volume provides digests of state laws on many subjects. Uniform subject headings are used under each state. Most of the summaries, written by lawyers, include the citations to the state statute.

*Shepard's Acts and Cases by Popular Names, Federal and State*. 2d ed. Colorado Springs, CO: Shepard's, 1979– .

Discussed earlier, this resource is mentioned here because it does index statutes of all states and can be used to locate similar legislation from state to state.

### Municipal Statutes

Municipal or local governments operate under powers granted to them by the state. Their legislative activities center on (1) a charter which is analogous to a state constitution; (2) ordinances, the legislative enactments of the local city council or board of supervisors; and (3) a code which arranges ordinances in force in some logical form. Few city codes are annotated. Working directly with such primary sources is usually necessary for legal research at the local level.

If a municipal library exists in your town, either as a section of the public library or in an office at city hall, use its resources. If not, work with the city clerk or various department heads. Always remember that the smaller the unit of government, the less likely it is that information will be arranged in an easily accessible fashion.

## FEDERAL REGULATORY LAW

### Federal Administrative Agencies

Concerned with the public or private rights and obligations of private parties, administrative agencies are the result of governmental growth. Their authority, vested and controlled by legislative action or presidential executive order, promulgates faster and more efficient enforcement of public policy. First used by states during the last half of the nineteenth century, administrative agencies centered their activities on the regulation of private economic activity. The Depression and New Deal ushered in a watershed period in the growth of federal regulatory agencies, as they focused on economic recovery. By the 1960's and 1970's social regulation became a primary concern of administrative agencies. In spite of the anti-regulatory trend of the late 1970's and early 1980's, agencies continue to formulate and administer public policy through rules and regulations, to provide an adjudicative procedure through hearings, and to subject their regulatory functions to judicial review. Administrative agencies have various labels: boards, commissions, bureaus, offices, departments, divisions, or corporations.

## Administrative Rules and Regulations

Because rules and regulations passed by administrative agencies have the effect of law, impact heavily upon private lives, and are constantly changing, it is imperative to have effective access to current rules and regulations.

### *Chronological Publication*

*Federal Register*. Washington, DC: U.S. Government Printing Office, 1936– . Daily.

Administrative agency issuance of rules is a fairly simple process. For any administrative rule or regulation to become effective it must be published first in the *Federal Register*. Thus the *Federal Register* is the administrative agencies' counterpart to Congress' *Statutes at Large*. Both include new statements of law as it occurs but are not useful for compiling rules or statutes by subject. The *Federal Register* differs from the *Statutes* because it also includes proposed actions.

The *Federal Register* is published daily Monday through Friday and indexed monthly, quarterly, and annually. Available online: *Dialog*, *SDC*.

### *Subject Publication*

*Code of Federal Regulations* (*CFR*). Office of the Federal Register. National Archives and Records Service. Washington, DC: U.S. Government Printing Office, 1936– . Annual.

In order to arrange federal regulations and amendments in force by subject, they are entered into the *Code of Federal Regulations*, published in fifty titles, with each title updated once a year. Besides a cumulated index, each title volume has its own index, plus a detailed table of contents. What has been said about using law books is certainly applicable here. Regulations tend to be indexed under their broader aspects. Plan to spend extra time exploring *CFR* tables of contents and indexes. Both *CFR* and *Federal Register* are available in microformat.

### *Keeping Current*

*List of CFR Sections Affected*. Office of the Federal Register. National Archives and Records Service. Washington, DC: U.S. Government Printing Office, 1936– . Monthly.

The currency of each title of *CFR* depends upon the date. Each year titles 1 through 16 are revised as of January 1; titles 17 through 27, April 1; titles 28 through 41, July 1; and titles 42 through 50, October 1. If regulations have been added, amended, or revoked, such changes will be noted in the monthly *List of CFR Sections Affected* or in "Cumulative List of Parts Affected," which is printed in the *Federal Register*.

*CIS Federal Register Index*. Bethesda, MD: Congressional Information Service, 1984– .

Its weekly publication allows this index to promptly demystify the complexity of the *Federal Register*. Proposed rules, rules, and notices of agencies responsible for developing and implementing Federal regulations are indexed in detail by subject and names, including issuing agencies, geographic areas, chemical substances, popular names of authorizing legislation, names of industries, organizations, corporations and individuals. Other indexes are by *CFR* section numbers and by federal agency docket numbers.

## STATE AND MUNICIPAL REGULATIONS

Rules and regulations of state agencies tend to follow the same publication schedule as federal sources. Regulations first appear in a chronological format, then are compiled into a subject, or title, arrangement. Publication of state agency regulations varies greatly across the states.

Regulations of municipal agencies often are acted upon by the legislative body of the municipality and hence incorporated into the ordinances and code. Others appear in such documents as policy manuals, either cumulated for various agencies or issued for a single agency.

Your sources for help in locating state and municipal regulations continue to be a state legal guide; a state or municipal library; the state or municipal agency; the Shepard's citations listed earlier; and, as always, your librarian.

## CASE LAW

Case law is that law which evolves from judicial interpretations of the constitution, the statutes, and the regulations. These judicial interpretations are rendered only when a case is brought before a court on appeal. A case may have majority, minority, concurring, and dissenting opinions.

Case law, like statute and regulatory law, follows a logical publication pattern, although some of its forms may be less familiar to you.

### Chronological Publication: Reporters

Reporters contain the written decisions of the courts in cases brought to them on appeal. Published chronologically, they are the primary sources—the building blocks—of case law. Decisions are usually published first in slip format soon after they are rendered and then in bound volumes at the end of each court term. There are separate sets of reporters for the various levels of federal and state courts and for groups of states.

Reporters, arranged by jurisdiction and by date of decision, are thus equivalent to *Statutes at Large*. Each volume lists the cases contained, and most also contain an alphabetical case name index. These indexes, however, do not cumulate; thus, if you do not know the year in which your case was decided (as well as the court), you will have to go through hundreds of individual reporter indexes to locate the case.

Court decisions may be published directly by the governmental jurisdiction concerned, in which case they are called *official reporters*, or by a commercial publisher, in which case they are called *unofficial reporters*. In some instances, a commercially published set has been designated by the jurisdiction to be its official reporter. In general, unofficial reporters contain helpful additional information such as reference aids, additional summaries, and referrals to related material in other publications, which do not appear in the official reporters. However, the actual case decisions, with any minority, majority, or concurring opinions, must, obviously, be identical.

### *United States Supreme Court*

*United States Reports*. Washington, DC: U.S. Government Printing Office.

The official reporter.

*United States Supreme Court Reports: Lawyers' Edition*. Rochester, NY: Lawyers' Co-op.

Decisions to 1956.

*United States Supreme Court Reports: Lawyers' Edition*. 2nd series. Rochester, NY: Lawyers' Co-op.

Decisions since 1956.

*Supreme Court Reporter*. St. Paul, MN: West.

All Supreme Court decisions.

Kurland, Philip B., and Gerhard Casper, eds. *Landmark Briefs and Arguments of the Supreme Court of the United States*. Frederick, MD: University Publications of America, 1978– .

This set includes the most significant Supreme Court decisions from 1793 to date. Its special value is that in addition to reprinting the actual decisions, it also includes the lawyers' briefs on both sides, amicus curiae briefs, many supporting documents, and the oral arguments before the court. The set is available in both bound volumes and on microfiche.

*United States Law Week*. Washington, DC: Bureau of National Affairs, 1932– .

Since it is published weekly, this is useful for finding the most recent decisions.

### *Lower Federal Courts*

Among the reporters for the lower federal courts are:

*Federal Reporter*. 2d series. St. Paul, MN: West, .

*Federal Supplement*. St. Paul, MN: West, .

### *State Reporters*

Every state has ensured that its appealed court decisions be published in some form. Some states publish their own; others rely on commercial publications.

*National Reporter System*. St. Paul, MN: West, 1879– .

This is a mammoth system for reporting state and federal court decisions in a series of regional and national reporters. State decisions can be found in the *Atlantic Reporter*, *North Western Reporter*, *North Eastern Reporter*, *Pacific Reporter*, *South Eastern Reporter*, *South Western Reporter*, and the *Southern Reporter*. In some instances coverage provided by the *National Reporter System* duplicates that available in official reporters; in others it is the only source.

## Subject Publication: Digests

A digest is a form of publication unique to case law. Digests are subject arrangements of summaries of the points of law discussed in each decision.

There are typically several points of law discussed in a court decision. Digests summarize each of these individual points for each case and then arrange the summaries by subject, in one encyclopedic alphabetical arrangement. In order to keep the digest current without reprinting the entire set, pocket parts are issued regularly for each volume.

Unlike codes, which are subject arrangements of laws or regulations and are designed to be used alone, digests should never be used alone in the study of case law. Digests do not contain the entire case; they are designed to be used as subject indexes to the reporters.

Most digests have two indexes:

1. A subject, or word, index, which leads to the areas within the digest where points at issue from relevant cases are summarized. In practice this index works in the same way as the index to an encyclopedia; it leads you to information about a subject;
2. A case name index which lists each of the cases summarized in that digest, gives the complete citation, and gives the subject areas within the digest where elements from that case are summarized.

It is helpful to remember the dual function of the case name index to the digest: if you know the name of the case and want to locate other cases which discuss the same topic, it will lead you to the proper section of the digest; if you know the name of the case, and need the citation, it will provide it. Note that the index volumes as well as the digest volumes have pocket parts.

### *Federal Digests*

*U.S. Supreme Court Reports Digest: Lawyers' Edition.* Rochester, NY: Lawyers' Co-op.

Indexes all Supreme Court cases.

*U.S. Supreme Court Digest.* St. Paul, MN: West.

Indexes all Supreme Court cases.

*West's Federal Practice Digest 2d.* St. Paul, MN: West.

Indexes lower federal court decisions from 1961 to 1975. Cases prior to that date are covered in earlier sets in this series.

*West's Federal Practice Digest 3d.* St. Paul, MN: West.

Indexes lower federal court decisions since 1975.

### *State Digests*

Digests for state court decisions are available from various sources. If your interest is in a single state, it is simplest to use the digest system for that particular state; most states have them. If your interest is somewhat broader or a separate digest is not available for the state with which you are concerned, the regional digests, published by West and corresponding to the regional reporter series, would be the best choice.

### *American Digest System*

The *American Digest System* is an overwhelmingly comprehensive digest system which attempts to cover every reported case in every jurisdiction in the country from 1658 to date. Published by West, it currently has about 350 volumes in ten series. Its bulk and comprehensiveness make it difficult to use, so that most criminal justice researchers will only turn to it after trying either an individual state or a regional digest. Perhaps its most useful and interesting series is the *Century Edition*, which purports to digest every reported American case from 1658 to 1896, in fifty volumes.

## SHEPARDIZING

Shepard's is a company that publishes a series of books called *citators*, each of which is keyed to one of the basic publications of the law. *Shepardizing* is a process that enables the researcher to determine if a specific case, statute, regulation, or ordinance has been discussed, cited, overturned, repealed, or affirmed. There are Shepard's citators for case, statute, and regulatory law on the municipal, state, and federal levels; all are published in confusingly identical maroon bindings and are kept up-to-date by supplements and advance sheets.

In appearance, citators are like no other form of publication in the world.

Consisting of columns of numbers, abbreviations, and arcane symbols, they appear to be exceedingly difficult, if not impossible, to use.

If you need to use a citator however, take heart. They are not nearly as difficult as they look; most people can master them fairly quickly by reading the introduction or getting a few minutes of instruction from the librarian. The key to understanding them is to use them.

## DISCUSSIONS ABOUT THE LAW

### Encyclopedias

When researching legal topics think of using encyclopedias in the same fashion as you would for other topics. Look to them to provide overviews, general orientations to topics with which you are not familiar, and for specific pieces of information such as dates, sponsors, and summaries or discussions of particular statutes or cases.

There are two groups of encyclopedias that can be helpful to the criminal justice researcher with need for information about the law: those written to meet the needs of nonlawyers and those, traditionally called legal encyclopedias, written specifically for the legal profession.

If your need for legal information is peripheral to your main topic, or if you are totally unacquainted with the legal issues that you are researching, it might be easiest to start with one of the encyclopedias designed for the nonlawyer.

*Guide to American Law* and the *Encyclopedia of Crime and Justice* will both provide factual information and broad overviews without the use of legal jargon. Both contain bibliographies, give citations to relevant cases and statutes, and include case name indexes which are helpful in locating summaries and discussions of specific cases. They are discussed in greater detail in chapter V.

*Corpus Juris Secundum*, published by West, and *American Jurisprudence, 2d*, published by Lawyers' Co-op, are the standard encyclopedias of the legal profession. Like other encyclopedias, they have a basic alphabetical subject arrangement, with a separate subject index for the set.

The most efficient approach to these encyclopedias is to use the general index to locate the article and then carefully scan the analytical table of contents which will be found at the beginning of most of the articles. These detailed lists of the contents of each article will help pinpoint precisely those pages that will be most helpful to you.

These encyclopedias do not contain case table or statute indexes and thus cannot be used easily to locate discussions and summaries of specific cases. They are designed for a subject approach.

Both of the traditional legal encyclopedias are updated by pocket parts, with individual volumes being occasionally reprinted. If there is a choice between these two sets, *American Jurisprudence, 2d* will probably be preferable, since the basic volumes are more up-to-date, and the typeface is easier to read.

Don't be intimidated by the appearance of a legal encyclopedia. A typical page will have dozens of closely packed footnotes, often taking up more than half the page; these footnotes cite the cases and statutes that have been used as the basis of the discussion. If you want only an overview of the topic, ignore the footnotes.

### Legal Periodicals

Legal periodicals, some of which are called law reviews, are like other scholarly or professional periodicals; they contain articles written for the specialist. As with other periodicals, the best way to locate an article on a particular topic is through the use of periodical indexes.

*Index to Legal Periodicals* and *Current Law Index* are the two most important indexes to legal journals. Both contain case name indexes which are extremely useful in trying to locate discussions of specific cases.

Online searching for periodical and newspaper articles about law is available. *Legal Resources Index*, available through *Dialog*, includes the data available from the printed *Current Law Index*, plus a number of legal newspapers and additional law reviews not included in *Current Law Index*. *Index to Legal Periodicals* is available online through *Wilsonline*. These indexes are discussed more fully in Chapter VIII.

## GUIDES TO LEGAL RESEARCH

The following two books, written for nonlawyers interested in legal research, will be particularly helpful to those with no experience in using legal resources:

Lewis, Alfred J. *Using Law Books*. Dubuque, IA: Kendall/Hunt, 1976.

Elias, Stephen. *Legal Research: How to Find and Understand the Law*. Berkeley, CA: Nolo Press, 1982.

Fuller discussions of legal research can be found in the many books written for law students. Among the most widely used is:

Jacobstein, J. Myron, and Roy M. Mersky. *Fundamentals of Legal Research*. 2d ed. Mineola, NY: Foundation Press, 1981.

# XIII

# Historical Research with Primary Sources: Nineteenth-Century America

What and how much did our ancestors think about criminal behavior? How did they define it? How did they dispense justice, punish the offender, or reform the delinquent? Was criminal behavior viewed by the public as common or uncommon? Did they believe it could be eradicated or that it would always be with them? Were some people destined to be criminal?

Some of the answers to these questions may be found in the titles below:

"On the Effects of Secluded and Gloomy Imprisonment on Individuals of the African Variety . . . ," *Journal of Prison Discipline and Philanthropy* (1847); "Crime and Pauperism," *DeBows Review* (1854); "Jury Trial," *North American Review* (1860); "Whippers and Anti-Whippers," *Journal of Prison Discipline and Philanthropy* (1850); "Increase of Crime in the U.S.," *Evangelical Review* (1860); "Juvenile Depravity," *Christian Examiner* (1825, 1830, 1849); "Gasocution," *Scientific American* (1893); "Care of Truants and Incorrigibles," *National Education Association Proceedings* (1894); "Report on the Ohio Penitentiary," *Moral Advocate* (1821).

## PRIMARY SOURCES AND SECONDARY SOURCES

One can learn about criminal justice history by selecting from among the many fine, recent books and articles that have been published on the subject. Perhaps a more interesting way is to read some of the primary sources upon which the secondary literature is based. This is not to say that every researcher should undertake large-scale historical research. Using historical sources, looking at a century-old annual report, reading the proceedings of the first conference of the American Correctional Society, browsing through the magazines and newspapers in which our great, great grandparents expressed their opinions on the social problems of the day—each can be such an interesting experience that it is worth trying by anyone who has the opportunity. Both beginning and experienced researchers often find it surprisingly satisfying.

The primary-source versus secondary-source issue is much clearer when considering historical studies than it is when dealing with present-day research. If the item was written at the time you are investigating, there is more confidence that it is a primary source; if it was written later it is almost always a secondary source. As with research on today's problems, the closer the source is to the event the greater its authority.

The purpose of this chapter is to introduce some of these primary sources to those unacquainted with them. For reasons of space, general interest, and availability of materials, this discussion will be limited to selected sources for the study of criminal justice in the United States during the nineteenth and early twentieth centuries.

For centuries the use of primary sources for historical research was limited to individuals who had the time and finances for long trips away from home and the credentials which would allow them access to rare and often fragile documents. Today, due to the wonders of micropublication and the efforts of reprint publishers, many primary sources (including all those discussed in this chapter) are widely available and can be used as easily by beginning undergraduates as by experienced researchers. If the particular item you wish to consult is not in your own library or another library in your area, it will be available through interlibrary loan.

## STRATEGIES FOR THE USE OF PRIMARY SOURCES

The basic strategy for using primary sources, either contemporary or historical, is the old adage "read between the lines."

- Who was the document written for? Who was it written by?
- All the information included in the document, whether true, partially true, or untrue, is obviously of some significance; the information not included may be of equal significance.
- The document should be examined for implicit assumptions; did the original readers know or assume things that are not immediately obvious to you? For example, decisions about how to organize police forces in mid-nineteenth-century American cities were often very political ones. The researcher needs to be aware of the political undertones of such decisions.
- The document can be analyzed on two levels: for the meaning it had to its contemporaries and for the additional insight that can be brought to it through a knowledge of what happened later.

In attempting to uncover the real content of a primary source, comparisons can frequently yield great insights. Wherever possible, consider comparing:

- a series of documents, for example, annual reports of a particular state prison system, across a number of years;
- annual reports of similar systems in different parts of the country for the same years;
- newspaper or periodical reports about a particular institution with the official reports of that institution;
- newspapers or periodical articles on a topic (youth gangs, capital punishment, prison labor, lynching) for different time periods or for the same period in different parts of the country;
- what was said about these topics in professional conferences compared to what was said in the popular press.

The basic publication formats of the nineteenth century were similar to those with which we are familiar. However, there were fewer of them, and most were written by and for people with less rigidly defined specializations and interests than is true today. The following types of sources will be discussed: periodical articles, reports and documents, newspapers, conference proceedings, books, and archives.

## PERIODICAL ARTICLES

Periodical articles are probably the most widely available group of sources and in many ways may be the most satisfying to use.

### Nineteenth-Century Criminal Justice Periodicals

*Journal of Prison Discipline and Philanthropy*. 1845–1920. Wilmington, DE: Scholarly Resources. Microfilm.

Printed in Pennsylvania, this was a substantial and long-lived publication, with close ties to organizations devoted to prison reform. Although a nineteenth-century tone of moral uplift is clearly evident, especially in the early period, the general orientation of this periodical reflects an increasingly professional outlook. It contains complete reprints of many official documents and summaries of others, original articles, and reprints of articles, sermons, and speeches, as well as news reports of interest to its readers. Items are from all over the Old World, as well as the New.

*Moral Advocate: A Monthly Publication on War, Duelling, Capital Punishment, and Prison Discipline*. Vols. 1–3, March 1821–1824. Ann Arbor, MI: University Microfilms International. Microfilm.

A short-lived publication whose basic tone is reflected in its title, this was largely the work of one man and was published in Mt. Pleasant, Ohio. Issues contained original articles, reprints from other magazines, both American and foreign, news reports of relevant activities, extracts of sermons and speeches, and summaries of reports from prisons and agencies in many states, as well as extensive reports on Ohio prisons.

*National Police Gazette*. 1845–1906. Ann Arbor, MI: University Microfilms International. Microfilm.

Originally a gazette was a government journal reporting official news. The concept of a gazette as a way of officially reporting crimes goes back at least to eighteenth-century England; in the nineteenth century the term *gazette* was adopted by commercial publishers. For some years the *National Police Gazette* did contain official lists of army deserters, but it was part of the sensationalist crime press and never a government document.

The value of this periodical for the researcher is as a picture of popular attitudes toward crime and sensationalism. In the first few years emphasis was placed on violent crime and criminal biographies, but there was a gradual movement toward greater concern with prostitution, and other salacious topics. Occasional appearance of a police blotter and some statistics could be useful in getting a picture of types and numbers of reported crimes.

Some sample headlines give the flavor of the *Gazette*: "A Brutal Assault; A Gang of Grain Laborers Attack One of Their Number; He is Beaten Unmercifully, and His Ear Bit Off; The Perpetrators of the Outrage Still at Large" (December 8, 1866, page 3); "A New York Pugilist Set Upon by Rowdies; He is Beaten and Almost Cut to Pieces in a Brothel; Not Expected to Survive" (September 21, 1867, page 3); "Audacity's Acme; A Wealthy Lady Assaulted, Garroted and Robbed of Her Diamond Earing [*sic*] on Fifth Avenue; In Broad Daylight; Amid a Throng of People, Who, with Her Companion are Paralyzed by the Bold Attack of the Thief" (March 1, 1879, page 11).

The journal is illustrated with woodcuts, some of which are exceedingly fine.

## Indexes to Nineteenth-Century General Interest Popular Periodicals

Among the hundreds of popular general interest periodicals published in the nineteenth century there were many concerned with issues of crime, justice, and law and order. The keys to locating these articles, including most of those listed at the beginning of this chapter, are these two indexes:

*Poole's Index to Periodical Literature, 1802–1906*. 6 vols. Rev. ed., reprinted. Gloucester, MA: Peter Smith, 1958.

Mr. Poole began compiling his index in 1848. The third edition of the basic volume, covering 1802 to 1881, was published in 1882 and is the basis for the reprint edition. Although not difficult to use, the indexing does not have the consistency or uniformity which we have come to expect in periodical indexes; use with care and imagination.

*19th Century Readers' Guide to Periodical Literature*. 2 vols. New York: H. W. Wilson, 1944.

Covering only the period from 1880 to 1900, this index was actually compiled in 1944 and is identical in format and indexing policies to the *Readers' Guide* with which you are familiar.

### Indexes to Nineteenth-Century Scholarly Periodicals

The development of scholarly disciplines in the nineteenth century and the related development of publications written exclusively by and for academics have been briefly described in the introduction to this book. Many of these early academic periodical articles can be located through use of the sets described below. Articles written during the time period you are researching can be considered primary sources if they document contemporary events; secondary sources if they describe those of earlier periods.

*CRIS: Combined Retrospective Index to Journals in History, 1838–1974.* 11 vols. Washington, DC: Carrollton Press, 1977.

*CRIS: Combined Retrospective Index to Journals in Political Science, 1886–1974.* 8 vols. Washington, DC: Carrollton Press, 1977.

See especially volume III, *Public Administration*, and the section on crime and law within that volume.

*CRIS: Combined Retrospective Index to Journals in Sociology, 1895–1974.* 6 vols. Washington, DC: Carrollton Press, 1978.

See especially volume V, *Social Disorganization*, and volume II, part 2, *Institutions, Law, and Legal Systems*.

Nontraditional in form and appearance, these are computer-generated indexes which combine some of the advantages of computer searching with those of traditional printed indexes.

## NEWSPAPERS

The only American newspaper covering the period we are discussing for which both the newspaper and its index are widely available is the *New York Times*.

The *Times*, considerably more sensational in tone in its early days than it is now, has always shown an interest in crime and criminals, justice and punishment and has always made attempts at national coverage.

There are some frustrations involved in using the indexes for these early years due to inconsistent indexing policies and a constantly shifting arrangement of material into four, six, and sometimes as many as sixteen different alphabets for a single year. However, persistence and imagination in the use of the index will pay off.

As a daily newspaper the *Times* was primarily a recorder of events and seems to have carried few articles dealing with problems of crime in general, but the numbers of entries under specific topics such as "Murders," "Blackmails," "Poisonings," and "Assaults and Affrays"—with a cross-reference: "For those terminating fatally, see Murders"—are thought provoking and sobering. In addition, there is generally a considerable list of articles grouped conveniently around the word "prison," with the entries covering news from all over the country. Information about police is most often under the name of the city rather than the general heading of police.

## REPORTS AND DOCUMENTS

Annual reports may contain statistical information, narrative descriptions of conditions and events, case histories, organizational charts, illustrations, or financial statements. They may present the barest, briefest possible picture or go on and on for many pages. As sources of official information they are frequently as interesting for what is omitted as for what is included. Information presented, and not presented, needs to be carefully assessed. As we have said, comparing an annual report for a specific institution with newspaper and periodical articles dealing with that institution for the same period can be instructive, as can comparisons of reports for similar institutions in another state, or the same institution during another time period.

The most accessible group of relevant reports is:

*State Reports on Correction and Punishment, Poverty and Public Welfare, prior to 1930*. Milwood, NY: Kraus Microfilm, 1973. Microfiche.

Among the reports included in this series are: California State Board of Prison Directors, 1879–1930 (includes San Quentin and Folsom prisons); Colorado State Board of Pardons, 1893–1922; Georgia Board of Public Welfare, 1920–31, and Prison Commission, 1897–1930; Ohio Board of Commissioners for Reform Schools, 1856–1913, and the State Board of Pardons, 1893–22; and, from Massachusetts, the reports of the Agents for Aiding Discharged Prisoners, 1846–1929, the General Superintendent of Prisons Report Concerning Prison Labor, 1887–1900, and the Commission on Probation, 1909–1927.

Other annual reports, either complete or summarized, may be located through newspaper and periodical indexes. They may be listed either under the name of the institution or body, under the location, or under the more general subject. The two journals listed which were concerned specifically with prisons and prison reform regularly published excerpts and summaries from official annual reports.

There is as yet no historical series of police department annual reports available in microform. However, such reports in their original format are frequently available in public libraries and in the libraries of local historical societies. If you are interested in using them, talk to your reference librarian who will probably be able to give you some leads.

## CONFERENCE PROCEEDINGS

Conference reports have always served the same purpose: they reflect the current concerns of those people most active in the field. Criminal justice researchers are fortunate to have two sets of conference proceedings which began publication in the late nineteenth century.

American Correctional Association. Annual Congress on Corrections. *Proceedings, 1870–1946*. Milwood, NY: Kraus Reprint, 1975. Microfilm with printed index.

Particularly for the years prior to formation of the International Association of Chiefs of Police, these congresses were the forum for discussions of policing and law enforcement as well as corrections.

The index to this set is particularly good. Indexing level is that of a book rather than periodical articles; discussions as well as formal presentations are included.

Among the topics covered are: sterilization of criminals; political influence in prison administration; insanity plea; physical characteristics of criminal and degenerate; contract system of prison labor; recidivists; prisoners' aid associations; probation; and parole.

National Conference on Social Welfare. *Proceedings*. 1874– .

This organization, founded in 1874, has undergone numerous name changes. Known originally as the Conference on Boards of Public Charities, it has also been called Conference of Charities, Conference of Charities and Correction, and National Conference of Charities and Corrections. In 1917 the name was changed to National Conference of Social Work, and in 1956 the current name, National Conference on Social Welfare, was adopted.

The proceedings of the annual conference were published and distributed widely. In addition to the original bound versions of these proceedings, there are now several microform editions available, published with slight title variations. (New York: Datamics; Ann Arbor: University Microfilms; Westport, CT: Greenwood Press; Princeton: Princeton Microform.)

This organization had much broader interests than the American Correctional Association. Along with problems of criminality and prisons, members were concerned with paupers, public health, orphans, child welfare, delinquents, and what they called defectives (insane, crippled, blind, deaf, retarded, epileptic).

Each volume of the proceedings until 1913 contains a section labeled "Report from the States." This was information reported to the association by state officials. Arranged by state, the amount (and probably the reliability) of information varies considerably from state to state and from year to year. There are a considerable number of statistics, along with narrative descriptions for all the categories of concern.

Among the items that might be of interest are: from 1889, an entire section on "The Ideal Prison System for a State," which included a report from the standing committee, formal papers, plus a discussion on prison regulation and on personnel;

from 1899, a section on "Politics in Charitable and Correctional Institutions"; and from 1912, a paper by Professor Roscoe Pound on "Social Problems and the Courts" and one by the Honorable William McAdoo, former New York City Police Commissioner, on "Women Offenders in New York."

## BOOKS

Many of the most influential books published during the nineteenth and early twentieth centuries have been reprinted; others are still available in their original formats in larger public libraries, older university libraries, historical societies, and through interlibrary loan.

If you are interested in looking at primary sources in book form, the easist way to locate them is through lists of the reprint series. The major ones are *Foundations of Criminal Justice* (AMS Press), which includes a reprint of the 1867 *Report on the Prisons and the Reformatories of the United States & Canada . . .*, by E. C. Wines and T. W. Dwight; *The Patterson Smith Reprint Series* (Patterson Smith), which includes a reprint of the 1869 *Half Century with Juvenile Delinquents; or the New York House of Refuge & Its Times*, by B. K. Peirce; and the *Police in America* series (Arno Press), which includes a reprint of William McAdoo's 1906 *Guarding a Great City*. Complete lists of these series can be found in *Books in Series* (R. R. Bowker, 1980– ).

## ARCHIVES

Archives are the one form of material that are used only for historical research. Archives are the noncurrent working files and records of an organization, government, individual, or committee. They can contain correspondence, reports, budget information, memos, speeches, photographs; that is, anything that was either generated or received. The main principle of organization for an archive is that the material retain the same organization and arrangement that it had when it was in use.

A number of archives containing information of interest to the criminal justice researcher have been filmed commercially and are available through purchase or interlibrary loan.

Rockefeller University. Archives. *Bureau of Social Hygiene Project and Research Files, 1913–40*. Wilmington, DE: Scholarly Resources, 1979. Microfilm with printed guide.

The Bureau of Social Hygiene, founded and funded by John D. Rockefeller, sponsored research in the broad field of social hygiene, including health care, prostitution, alcoholism, crime, police, and penology. Reading through the various folders of correspondence and reports from 1913 to the mid–1930's when the Bureau's activity basically stopped, it seems that every famous name in the field of criminal justice appears: Sheldon Glueck, Roscoe Pound, Bruce Smith, Edwin

Sutherland, Raymond Fosdick, J. Edgar Hoover, Thorsten Sellin, George W. Wickersham.

Perhaps typical of the range of material to be found in this archive is folder 288, titled *Criminology, 1914–28*. It includes reports on the current status of crime statistics gathering, summaries of current criminological research, proposals for the development of major programs for research into criminal justice administration, questions and reports about the drop in British prison inmates in the preceding fifteen years, and correspondence and reports dealing with prison industries, police schools, and women police.

*University Settlement Society of New York City Papers*. Sanford, NC: Microfilming Corporation of America, 1972. Microfilm with printed guide.

The Bureau of Social Hygiene was involved in large-scale national and international projects; the province of the activities of the University Settlement Society was a neighborhood of perhaps several dozen square blocks. Yet they were concerned with many of the same issues.

The University Settlement was founded in 1891. Its goal was to alleviate the evils that resulted from concentrating large masses of poor, uneducated, unskilled immigrants within the densely populated, noisy, dirty, urban environment which was New York's Lower East Side at the time. Those concerned with juvenile delinquency, the relation of crime to poverty, and community crime prevention programs would find this archive of the correspondence, reports, and records of one of America's largest and oldest social settlements unparalleled in their richness.

## SOME HELPFUL REFERENCE BOOKS

The following books may be helpful in providing a quick orientation and some background information about the period being researched.

Bliss, William D. T., ed. *The Encyclopedia of Social Reform, including Political Economy, Political Science, Sociology, and Statistics, Covering Anarchism, Charities, Civil Service, Currency, Land and Legislation Reform, Penology, Socialism, Social Purity, Trades Unions, Woman Suffrage, etc.* Reprint of 1897 edition. Westport, CT: Greenwood Press, 1970.

This is probably the first English-language social science encyclopedia. The articles were written by many of the leading scholars and reformers of the period and are useful in giving an overview of the ideas and opinions of the late nineteenth century. Many of the longer articles include bibliographies.

Farmer, J. S., and W. E. Henley. *Slang and Its Analogues*. New York: Arno Press, 1970. Reprint of the seven-volume set issued 1890–1904.

Goldin, Hyman E., Frank O'Leary, and Morris Lipsius. *Dictionary of American Underworld Lingo*. Boston: Twayne, 1950.

Partridge, Eric. *The Macmillan Dictionary of Historical Slang*. New York: Macmillan, 1974.

Schlesinger, Arthur M., Jr., ed. *The Almanac of American History*. New York: G. P. Putnam's Sons, 1983.

Gives the highlights of American history in short, year-by-year sequences. Very useful for a fast orientation to the key issues in the news.

*The World Almanac*, 1868–1893. Cleveland, OH: Bell & Howell Microphoto Division, 1973. Microfiche.

Almanacs, because they are not written from an historical perspective, are useful for checking what was considered newsworthy in the year in which they were published. Almanacs of the nineteenth century, like those of today, also contain statistics, including many relating to crime and social problems, and biographies.

# XIV

# Resources for the Study of Criminal Justice in Other Countries

Studies of criminal justice systems in other countries are enlightening both for the information they give about those countries and for the perspective they can give about our own. Attitudes toward crime, as well as crime rates, vary greatly in different types of societies. Even within fairly similar industrialized western nations, there are great differences. Cross-national comparisons of crime and violence are one way of testing theories about crime causation and social control.

Although in recent years interest in such studies has been growing, comparative criminal justice research is still not easy due to the paucity of material, particularly in English. What is available is often widely scattered and ineffectively indexed or cataloged. Further complications arise because methods of gathering statistics vary greatly, and the reliability of such data varies even more.

This chapter will discuss materials specifically designed to aid research in comparative criminal justice and will also highlight those previously discussed sources most likely to be useful in research projects of this type. Strategies for the most efficient use of these sources in comparative studies will be pointed out.

## OVERVIEWS

For a reliable, one-volume orientation to the country you are researching, consult:

American University. Foreign Area Studies. *Area Handbook Series*. Washington, DC: U.S. Government Printing Office. Irregular.

There are volumes for most countries in the world. Revisions are constantly in preparation, so be sure to get the latest edition.

For overviews of various aspects of criminal justice in other countries, consult:

Cappelletti, Mauro, and Bryant Garth, eds. *Access to Justice: A World Survey*. 4 vols. Sijthoff & Noordhoff-Alphenaandenrijn, A. Giuffre, editor, Milan, 1978.

The report of the Florence Access-to-Justice project, the first two volumes of this set contain reports from China, Colombia, England, France, Germany, Holland, Hungary, Indonesia, Israel, Italy, Japan, Mexico, Poland, the Soviet Union, Spain, Sweden, the United States, and Uruguay. The title of the set is descriptive. Concern is with legal rights and the ability of citizens to obtain justice, not with law enforcement.

Cole, George F., Stanislaw J. Frankowski, and Marc G. Gertz, eds. *Major Criminal Justice Systems*. Beverly Hills, CA: Sage Publications, 1981.

Divided into common law, civil law, and socialist law countries, this provides brief overviews of the criminal justice systems in Canada, England, Germany (both East and West), Japan, Poland, the Soviet Union, Sweden, and the United States. Fairly extensive bibliographies are included.

*Encyclopedia of Crime and Justice*. See chapter V for full discussion. Many articles in this set include a comparative approach to their topics. However, geographic entries in the index are only given as subdivisions of subjects. There are no entries directly under the name of the country.

Johnson, Elmer H. *International Handbook of Contemporary Developments in Criminology*. 2 vols. Westport, CT: Greenwood Press, 1983.

The concern in these short overviews is with criminology and penology; law enforcement and police are not included. Almost every country in the world is covered.

Klein, Malcolm W., ed. *Western Systems of Juvenile Justice*. Beverly Hills, CA: Sage Publications, 1984.

Provides overviews and bibliographies for the United States, Canada, England and Wales, Israel, Holland, the Federal Republic of Germany, Denmark, and Sweden.

New York University. School of Law. Criminal Law Education and Research Center. *American Series of Foreign Penal Codes*. South Hackensack, NJ: Fred B. Rothman, 1960– .

This ongoing series now includes more than twenty countries. Each volume contains a rather substantial introduction discussing the historical evolution of the penal code, its general characteristics, structure, and highlights.

Redden, Kenneth Robert, ed. *Modern Legal Systems Cyclopedia*. 4 vols. Buffalo, NY: William S. Hein, 1984.

Covers the legal systems of almost every country in the world, including many of the smaller ones for which information is most difficult to locate. Information is given about the historical development of the governmental system, current national and local government structure, political parties, and systems for reporting legal decisions. Includes bibliographies.

Walker, David. *The Oxford Companion to Law*. Oxford: Clarendon, 1980.

A very useful one-volume encyclopedia devoted primarily to the law of Great Britain and western Europe. Included are substantial overview articles of the law in France, Spain, Great Britain, Germany, Italy, and the Islamic countries. Other entries include biographies, cases, and statutes. Bibliographies are included for some topics.

Walsh, Dermot, and Adrian Poole. *A Dictionary of Criminology*. London: Routledge & Kegan Paul, 1983.

A British publication, this volume will be particularly useful for those interested in Great Britain. Definitions are given for many uniquely British terms, as well as those of more international usage. Entries include identification of, and citations to, specific laws and cases. There are some bibliographies, mostly citing British sources.

Of the one-volume encyclopedias aimed at popular audiences, which are discussed in chapter V, the following are international in coverage: *The Murderers' Who's Who, Almanac of World Crime*, and *Look for the Woman*.

## BIBLIOGRAPHIES

In a field where locating adequate and appropriate information can be difficult, the importance of a good bibliography cannot be overstated. Make use of any printed bibliographies that are available, including those in the encyclopedic sources cited at the beginning of this chapter. Don't forget to check for bibliography subdivisions when using the library catalog.

Academy of Criminal Justice Sciences. *ACJS Curriculum and Course Development Project: International Criminal Justice Systems*. Omaha, NE: Academy of Criminal Justice Sciences, 1984.

Countries covered are Australia, Canada, China, West Germany, Great Britain, Japan, the Soviet Union, and Sweden.

Each chapter is designed to serve as the basis for a full-semester course on one country. The extensive, high-quality bibliographies should be the first place to look for anyone interested in the countries covered. Also included are a sample course outline and, in some cases, a summary of the criminal justice system of the country.

Lagergren, Thomas R., and Kathleen A. Pitt. *International Criminology and Criminal Justice: A Selected Bibliography*. Washington, DC: U.S. Government Printing Office, 1977.

Shanley, Marc, and Marjorie Kravitz. *International Policing: A Selective Bibliography*. Rockville, MD: National Criminal Justice Reference Service, 1978.

Useful because all items listed are available from the National Criminal Justice Reference Service.

### Custom Bibliographies

In some instances a computer search may be the best way to compile a good bibliography of any size. This will be particularly true if you are interested in a specific topic within one country, for example, behavior modification programs in prisons in Sweden, or if you are interested in locating anything written about a country for which there is very little available material about any aspect of criminal justice. As we survey the best sources for comparative research we will indicate those that are available for online searching.

*Note*: When filling out your Computer Search Request Form, remember to include information about which languages you can read. This will help keep the cost of the search down and will avoid burdening you with citations that cannot be used.

## PERIODICAL INDEXES AND ABSTRACTS

See chapter VIII for full citations and discussions of these sources.

*Police Science Abstracts*.

*Criminology and Penology Abstracts*.

Both these services are international in coverage. Since they include a good deal of valuable comparative information, it is fortunate that they are simple to use; just check under the name of the country in which you are interested. Be alert to languages however; all the abstracts are in English, even in cases where the article itself is not.

*Criminal Justice Periodical Index*.

Although this includes only English-language journals, there is still some information about other countries. Unlike the two indexes discussed above, however, the information will be found listed not directly under the name of the country but as a geographic subheading under the specific subject; for instance, Murder–Great Britain.

*Criminal Justice Periodical Index* is available online. Although its use online is not recommended for most searches since it is simple to use in the print format, if you are looking for comparative information and want citations for all articles dealing with a specific country, an online search would be most efficient.

*Criminal Justice Abstracts*.

Another service including information about foreign countries from English-language journals only. Coverage here is quite selective with fairly long and informative abstracts. Some report literature is included along with periodical articles.

This is fast to check since the index gives access directly by country name, as well as through the subject. Not available online.

*Public Affairs Information Service (PAIS).*

The online version of this index includes substantial numbers of foreign periodicals, some of which publish in English. The print version of *PAIS* comes in two parts: the *PAIS Bulletin* and the *PAIS Foreign Language Index.*

*Psychological Abstracts and Psychinfo.*

*Psychological Abstracts* has worldwide coverage. For information about other countries the online version, *PsychInfo*, is preferable to the print version which does not make entries under country names.

## PERIODICALS

There are several periodicals that specialize in comparative coverage. Although their contents are accessible through indexes, it is frequently worthwhile to browse through recent issues to see the direction of current research or to get ideas for your own research. Most likely to be useful are:

*International Criminal Police Review*. St. Cloud, France: International Criminal Police Organization, 1946– . Monthly.

The official publication of the International Criminal Police Organization (Interpol), with editions published in English, Spanish, French, and Arabic. Unlike other publications in this area, this is a professional journal, not an academic one. It contains short articles and news notes about law enforcement and criminal investigation in many different countries, written for working law enforcement officials. Easiest access is through *Police Science Abstracts*, although it also has its own yearly index.

*International Journal of Comparative and Applied Criminal Justice*. Wichita, KS: Wichita State University. Vol. 1– , 1977– . Biannual.

The title of this journal accurately reflects its content. All aspects of criminal justice are covered. It is indexed in *Criminal Justice Periodical Index* but makes worthwhile browsing if your interests are broad.

## TRANSLATIONS OF FOREIGN-LANGUAGE INFORMATION SOURCES

Executive Office of the President. Foreign Broadcast Information Service. Joint Publications Research Service. *JPRS Translations*. Washington, DC: U.S. Government Printing Office, 1962– .

*TRANSDEX Index*. Wooster, OH: Bell & Howell. Vol. 9, 1970/71. (Vols. 1–8, 1962–69 published under title *Bibliography-Index to Current United States JPRS Translations*.)

In order to provide ready access to foreign-language material reflecting current concerns and activities in countries all over the world, the United States government publishes documents selected and translated by its Joint Publications Research Service. The documents are issued in several regional series.

Since currency of ideas and issues is of major concern to the publishers, most items translated are newspaper and magazine articles; some government documents are also included.

This is probably the single best available English-language source of information about current worldwide police activities.

The simplest access to this information is through the commercially published *TRANSDEX Index*. A keyword index which includes entries both under subject and country name, it is issued monthly in paper and cumulated annually on microfiche.

Large research libraries, particularly those with government document depositories, are most likely to have the complete set of translations and indexes. Many libraries may subscribe only to the indexes. Where the documents themselves are not readily available, they may be ordered on microfiche directly from the publisher of the index.

U.S. Department of Justice. National Institute of Justice. *International Summaries: A Collection of Selected Translations in Law Enforcement and Criminal Justice.* 1978–80 issued as a periodical. Since 1980 published irregularly as monographic documents.

Translations of articles and some documents. Indexed in the *Monthly Catalog*, both online and in print.

## NEWS SOURCES AND PUBLIC OPINION POLLS

The single best English-language source of newspaper articles about police and crime in foreign countries is the publication of the Joint Publications Research Service discussed earlier in this chapter.

The London *Times*, 1788– .

*Index to the Times of London*, 1906– . (Preceded by *Palmer's Index to the Times Newspaper, 1790–1941*.)

The London *Times* has always shown considerably more interest in affairs of foreign countries than is characteristic of most American newspapers. The researcher will find fairly frequent use of subheadings such as riots and disturbances, crime, police, and prisons under the names of other countries in the London *Times* index.

Survey Research Consultants International. *Index to International Public Opinion*. Westport, CT: Greenwood Press, 1978/79– . Annual.

Publishes the results of important surveys conducted by leading opinion research organizations throughout the world. Surveys are arranged under broad subject areas, such as crime and justice. Indexes are by topic, by location where the survey was taken, and by geographic areas which are covered in the survey.

## DOCUMENTS

### United States Government Documents

*National Criminal Justice Reference Service.*

The rather nonselective quality of this data base, which includes books and articles as well as documents and reports, is a benefit to those doing comparative research, since the NCJRS net extends to materials about other countries. Despite the fact that it is limited to English-language materials published in the United States, it includes a considerable number of citations to information in various formats, including U.S. government documents, dealing with other countries.

Easiest access is through online searching, although a microfiche index is also available. See fuller discussion in chapter VII.

Other U.S. documents dealing with crime and justice in foreign countries can be located through *CIS/Annual* and the *Monthly Catalog*, both discussed in chapter VII.

### Foreign Government Documents

Documents issued by foreign governments, and available in English, are not easy to locate. Best sources would be *Public Affairs Information Service* online, *National Criminal Justice Service* online, and the *TRANSDEX Index* to publications of the Joint Publications Research Service.

### Documents of International Organizations

The primary source and distributor of international documents is the United Nations. Check the annual *Yearbook of the United Nations* for an overview of current issues under consideration. The following indexes will provide access to international documents.

*UNDOC: Current Index; United Nations Documents.* New York: United Nations Publications, 1979– . Ten issues per year.

*UNDOC*, successor to the *United Nations Documents Index* and *UNDEX*, indexes U.N. documents and publications received by the Dag Hammarskjold Library at U.N. headquarters in New York. If the library you are using includes U.N. documents in its regular collection, you will find them listed in the catalog. If the library maintains U.N. documents as a separate collection they will probably be arranged by the U.N. "symbol," another term for a call number. *UNDOC* can be helpful for international comparisons. Subjects range from prostitution to crime, international law, drug abuse, terrorism, bombings, imprisonments, law enforcement, and administration of justice. Non-U.N. publications received at the U.N. library are listed in a monthly index called *Current Bibliographic Information.*

*International Bibliography, Information, Documentation: Publications of International Organizations.* New York: UNIPUB, 1973– . Quarterly.

Annotated entries note publications, including periodicals and their tables of contents. Subject indexes list items under broad classifications such as "drugs" and "drug abuse," "courts and tribunals," and "crime and juvenile delinquency." Includes an index by title. If your library is small it may not own many of these items. Remember interlibrary loan.

Reno, Edward A. *League of Nations Documents, 1919–1946: A Descriptive Guide and Key to the Microfilm Collection*. 3 vols. New Haven, CT: Research Publications, 1973–75.

This source will be tapped only if you are doing an historical study. Both documents and serials publications of the League of Nations are noted. Sections on "social questions" and "legal questions" can be mined for information of interest to criminal justice researchers.

## STATISTICAL SOURCES

Archer, Dane, and Rosemary Gartner. *Violence and Crime in Cross-National Perspective*. New Haven, CT: Yale University Press, 1984.

About half of this book contains what the authors call their Comparative Crime Data File. In over 250 pages of small print we are given statistics for murder, manslaughter, homicide, rape, assault, robbery, and theft from 110 countries and 44 cities, from 1900 to 1974. Availability of statistics naturally varies; in some cases (for example, Bolivia), we are given only one year; in other cases there are very complete runs available, with Chile, Scotland, and Sri Lanka (Ceylon) having the longest continuous series. Each table gives the absolute figure, rate per 100,000, and the population of the country for the year. These, like most statistics, need to be used with care.

*Current National Statistical Compendiums*. Washington, DC: Congressional Information Service, 1970–

This is a collection, on microfiche, of statistical yearbooks from over one hundred countries, many of which include data on crime and corrections. The publisher regularly adds new editions of the yearbooks as they become available. Many of the yearbooks include English translations, although the alphabetical arrangement will generally be according to the original language. Where there is no translation, a dictionary can generally give sufficient help to enable the statistical tables to be understandable.

The reliability of the data in this series varies considerably, as does its currency. The figures need to be used with great care; there are scholars who contend that crime statistics reported by some foreign governments are totally suspect. Use of these statistics to compare nations is exceedingly difficult since definitions and methods of counting vary widely.

*Index to International Statistics* (IIS). Washington, DC: Congressional Information Service, 1983– . Monthly.

An index to statistics issued by international organizations, including the United Nations. See chapter X for a complete discussion.

*International Crime Statistics*. Paris: International Criminal Police Organization, 1950/51– . Irregular.

These volumes are issued irregularly and slowly. Although Interpol has 135 member countries, only a limited number supply statistics for this publication. As with so many other sources, this tool has very limited usefulness in making comparisons between nations because of wide variations in definitions, methods of collection, and reliability of reported figures.

## BOOKS

The library catalog, although frequently frustrating for those interested in comparative criminal justice, is one of the best tools available. Following are some guidelines for its use in this area.

Books dealing with criminal justice topics in other countries are listed under the topic, with a subdivision for the country, and not directly under the name of the country; for example, Correctional institutions–Sweden; Law Enforcement–Japan.

If the book deals with the topic in a specific city, it may be under the name of the city, under the topic with a subdivision for the city, or under the topic with a subdivision for the country, followed by the city.

If a book deals with the topic in only two countries, it will be given two subject headings, reflecting both places. For example, a book about police in France and England will have two headings: Police–France and Police–England.

If the book deals with more than two countries, it will be given the next most general heading; for example, a book comparing the police in France, Germany, and Italy: Police–Europe; but a book comparing police in France, Japan, and the United States: Police. In some cases such works may be given the heading Criminal Justice, Administration of—Comparative Studies. Books that deal exclusively with legal materials, will be given the subject heading Comparative law. These are cataloging policies that clearly make it difficult to locate comparative criminal justice materials in most library catalogs and explains the emphasis given earlier in this chapter on utilizing printed bibliographies wherever available.

# Appendix A

# Selected Lists of Library of Congress Subject Headings in Criminal Justice

There are several ways in which subject headings may be alphabetized. Arrangement in the catalog you are using may vary from that shown here.

## CORRECTIONS

Afro-American prisoners
Amnesty
Bail
Capital punishment
Chaplains, prison
Children of prisoners
Children of women prisoners
Church work with prisoners
Collective bargaining–correctional institutions
Convict labor
Convict ships
Correctional institutions
Correctional institutions–costs
Correctional institutions–design and construction
Correctional institutions–fires and fire prevention
Correctional institutions–standards
Correctional law
Correctional personnel
Correctional psychology
Corrections
Corrections–administration

Corrections–contract services
Corrections–cost effectiveness
Corrections–data processing
Corrections–evaluation
Corrections–finance
Corrections–history
Corrections–research
Corrections–standards
Death row
Detention of persons
Electrocution
Escapes
Ex-convicts
Ex-convicts–employment
Ex-convicts–legal status, laws, etc.
Ex-convicts–mental health
Ex-convicts–services for
Executions and executioners
False imprisonment
Group homes for children
Halfway houses
Hanging
Imprisonment
Imprisonment–psychological aspects
Imprisonment–social aspects
Indeterminate sentence
Information storage and retrieval systems–corrections
Inmate guards
Interviewing in corrections
Juvenile corrections
Juvenile delinquents–rehabilitation
Juvenile delinquents–services for
Juvenile detention homes
Juvenile justice, administration of
Juvenile parole
Juvenile probation
Legal assistance to prisoners
Life imprisonment
Mexican-American prisoners
Open prisons
Pardon
Parole
Parole officers
Penal colonies
Political prisoners
Pre-release programs for prisoners
Pre-sentence investigation reports
Pre-trial intervention

Pre-trial release
Preventive detention
Prison administration
Prison contraband
Prison discipline
Prison furloughs
Prison homicide
Prison hospitals
Prison hulks
Prison industries
Prison libraries
Prison physicians
Prison psychology
Prison reformers
Prison release gratuities
Prison riots
Prison sentences
Prison violence
Prison wardens
Prisoners
Prisoners–attitudes
Prisoners–classification
Prisoners–drug use
Prisoners–education
Prisoners–health and hygiene
Prisoners–legal status, laws, etc.
Prisoners–medical care
Prisoners–personal narratives
Prisoners–psychiatric care
Prisoners–recreation
Prisoners–services for
Prisoners-sexual behavior
Prisoners–suicidal behavior
Prisoners as artists
Prisoners as authors
Prisoners' families
Prisoners' songs
Prisoners' wives
Prisoners' writings
Prisons
Prisons–construction
Prisons–employees
Prisons–laws and regulations
Prisons–military
Prisons–missions and charities
Prisons–officials and employees
Prisons–overcrowding
Prisons–religious life

Prisons–sanitation
Prisons–security measures
Prisons–visits and correspondence with inmates
Prisons, coeducational
Probation
Probation officers
Punishment
Punishment in crime deterrence
Recidivists
Reformatories
Reformatories for women
Rehabilitation of criminals
Rehabilitation of juvenile delinquents
Sentences (criminal procedure)
Social work with delinquents and criminals
Strikes and lockouts–prisons
Trade unions–correctional personnel
Volunteer workers in corrections
Women correctional personnel
Women prisoners
Women prisoners–sexual behavior
Work release of prisoners
Workhouses

**CRIME AND CRIMINALS**

Abused wives
Adultery
Afro-American criminals
Aged–crimes against
Aged offenders
Alcoholism and crime
Anarchism and anarchists
Arson
Arson investigation
Art thefts
Assassinations
Assassins
Assault and battery
Automobile thefts
Bank robberies
Bombings
Brigands and robbers
Burglary
Burglary protection
Buses–vandalism
Cargo theft
Castration of criminals and defectives

Child abuse
Child molesting
Church work with criminals
Church work with juvenile delinquents
Commercial crimes
Competency to stand trial
Computer crimes
Confessions (law)
Conjugal violence
Corruption investigation
Crime and age
Crime and criminals
Crime and criminals–biography
Crime and criminals–economic aspects
Crime and criminals–fiction
Crime and criminals–history
Crime and criminals–identification
Crime and criminals–political aspects
Crime and criminals–research
Crime and criminals–sex differences
Crime and criminals in literature
Crime and criminals in the Bible
Crime and superstition
Crime and the press
Crime and weather
Crime forecasting
Crime in television
Crimes aboard aircraft
Crimes aboard buses
Crimes without victims
Criminal anthropology
Criminal behavior, prediction of
Criminal intent
Criminal psychology
Criminal registers
Decriminalization
Drug abuse and crime
Education and crime
Electronics in crime prevention
Embassy buildings–takeovers
Embezzlement
Employee theft
Evidence, criminal
Family violence
Female offenders
Forgery
Fraud
Fugitives from justice

Gangs
Gangster films
Graffiti
Homicide
Hoodlums
Hostage negotiation
Hostages
Hypnotism and crime
Incest
Indecent assault
Indians of North America–crime
Infanticide
Insane, criminal and dangerous
Japanese American criminals
Jewel thieves
Jewish criminals
Juvenile delinquency
Juvenile delinquents
Juvenile delinquents' writings
Larceny
Local transit crime
Mafia
Mentally handicapped and crime
Military offenses
Mugging
Murder
Narcotics and crime
Narcotics dealers
Offenses against property
Offenses against public safety
Offenses against the person
Organized crime
Outlaws
Parapsychology and criminal investigation
Parricide
Pedophilia
Pickpockets
Pimps
Poisoning
Political crimes and offenses
Post-conviction remedies
Pre-trial release
Prison homicide
Prostitutes
Prostitution
Prostitution, juvenile
Racketeering
Rape

Rape in marriage
Rape victims
Rape victims–services for
Rapists
Robbery
Rogues and vagabonds
Rural crime
School vandalism
School violence
Securities theft
Sex and law
Sex crimes
Sex offenders
Shoplifting
Sodomy
Status offenders
Stealing
Sterilization of criminals and defectives
Suburban crimes
Subversive activities
Swindlers and swindling
Terrorism
Terrorists
Theft from motor vehicles
Thieves
Tongs (secret societies)
Train robberies
Unemployment and crime
Uxoricide
Vandalism
Vice
Victims of crime
Violence–research
Violent crimes
Violent deaths
Volunteer workers in criminal justice administration
War and crime
White-collar crimes
Wife abuse
Women–crimes against
Women terrorists
Youth crime and unemployment
Youth–crimes against

## POLICE AND LAW ENFORCEMENT

Aeronautics in police work
Afro-American police

Arrest (police methods)
Assassination
Auxiliary police
Campus police
Chaplains, police
Child molesting–investigation
Collective bargaining–police
Collective labor agreements–police
Communication in police administration
Constables
Crime analysis
Crime laboratories
Crime prevention
Crime prevention–citizen participation
Crime prevention–economic aspects
Crime prevention and architectural design
Crime scene searches
Criminal investigation
Criminal jurisdiction
Criminal justice, administration of
Criminal justice, administration of–cross-cultural studies
Criminal justice personnel–training of
Criminal law
Criminal procedure
Criminologists
Dermatoglyphics
Detectives
Detectives in mass media
Discrimination in criminal justice administration
Electronics in crime prevention
Fingerprints
Firearms
Firearms–law and legislation
Footprints
Gun control
Harbor police
Informers
Insurance, police liability
Interviewing in law enforcement
Jewish police
Law enforcement
Law enforcement as a profession
Lie detectors and detection
Mounted police
Narcotic enforcement agents
Palmprints
Photography, legal
Police

Police–appropriations and expenditures
Police–assaults against
Police–attitudes
Police–bibliography
Police–complaints against
Police–contract services
Police–correspondence, reminiscences
Police–cost effectiveness
Police–data processing
Police–discipline
Police–diseases and hygiene
Police–examinations, questions, etc.
Police–family relationships
Police–height requirements
Police–history
Police–in-service training
Police–job stress
Police–labor productivity
Police–legal status, laws, etc.
Police–malpractice
Police–morality
Police–officials and employees
Police–personnel management
Police–physical training
Police–political activity
Police–public opinion
Police–recruiting
Police–residence requirements
Police–response time
Police–retirement
Police–safety measures
Police–salaries, pensions, etc.
Police–special weapons and tactics units
Police–study and teaching
Police–study and teaching (higher)
Police–supervision of
Police–uniforms
Police administration
Police and mass media
Police and minority groups
Police and the press
Police charges
Police chiefs
Police communication systems
Police corruption
Police discretion
Police divers
Police dogs

Police ethics
Police fire integration
Police legal advisors
Police murders
Police patrol
Police patrol–specialized units
Police power
Police professionalization
Police psychologists
Police psychology
Police pursuit driving
Police questioning
Police regulations
Police reports
Police services for juveniles
Police shooting ranges
Police shootings
Police social work
Police stations
Police supervision
Police surveys
Police training
Police vehicles
Police wives
Police, Black
Police, private
Police, rating of
Police, rural
Police, state
Policewomen
Public relations–police
Punishment in crime deterrence
Radar in speed limit enforcement
Railroad police
Riot helmets
Searches and seizures
Sex crimes–investigation
Sheriffs
Strikes and lockouts–police
Team policing
Tear gas
Television in police work
Trade unions–police
Traffic police
Undercover operations
Voiceprints
Volunteer workers in law enforcement
White-collar crime investigation

# Appendix B

# Some Useful Directories

A directory is a list of organized data such as names, addresses, or telephone numbers. Criminal justice researchers or practitioners frequently utilize such resources to contact others with similar interests or in similar positions. Directories prove especially useful for conducting surveys. Most are issued annually. This list of selected directories covers diverse aspects of criminal justice activities.

## AGENCIES AND ASSOCIATIONS

*Criminal Justice Agencies*. Justice Department, Washington, DC 20531.

This granddaddy of criminal justice directories, published in ten volumes in 1974–75, provides names and addresses for over fifty-seven thousand state and local agencies. Includes criminal and civil courts, probation and parole agencies, prison industries, and crime commissions.

*National Justice Agency List*. Bureau of Justice Statistics, Justice Department, Washington, DC 20531.

Reissue and update of *Criminal Justice Agencies*, now available on magnetic tape, microfilm, mailing labels, or computer printout.

*Directory of Law Enforcement and Criminal Justice Associations and Research Centers*. National Bureau of Standards, Commerce Department, Washington, DC 20234.

Listing of national, nonprofit, professional, and volunteer social action associations and research centers.

*World Directory of Criminological Institutes*. United Nations Social Defence Research Institute, 52 Via Guilia, 1–00186 Rome, Italy.

Notes areas of interest or study of 450 institutes, worldwide.

*Encyclopedia of Associations*. Gale Research Company, Book Tower, Detroit, MI 48226.

General guide to national and international nonprofit organizations in all fields.

## LAW ENFORCEMENT

*Directory of IACP Members and Buyers' Guide Issue*. International Association of Chiefs of Police, 13 Firstfield Road, Gaithersburg, MD 20878.

The September issue of *Police Chief* lists federal, state, local, and some county law enforcement personnel. Buyers' guide section notes manufacturers and distributors of police equipment.

*Directory of Sheriffs of the United States*. National Sheriffs' Association, 1250 Connecticut Avenue, Washington, DC 20036.

Information on three thousand one hundred sheriffs and others in federal, state, and county criminal justice work.

*National Directory of Law Enforcement Administrators and Correctional Institutions*. National Police Chiefs and Sheriffs Information Bureau, 152 W. Wisconsin Avenue, Milwaukee, WI 53203.

Listing by state of county and regional prosecutors; municipal and county police chiefs; state law enforcement personnel, correctional institutions, and top elected officials; and federal personnel and institutions.

*The Municipal Yearbook*. International City Management Association, 1120 G Street, NW, Washington, DC 20005.

This general municipal information source includes names and telephone numbers of police chiefs and departmental statistics, including salaries.

## COURTS

*United States Court Directory*. Administrative Office of the United States Court, Washington, DC 20402.

Judges, clerks, and circuit executives of 130 federal courts. Semiannual.

*Federal Court Directory*. Want Publishing, 1511 K Street, NW, Washington, DC 20005.

Similar to above. Includes appointment information for judges.

## CORRECTIONS

*Directory of Juvenile and Adult Correctional Departments, Institutions, Agencies and Paroling Authorities*; and *National Jail and Adult Detention Directory*. American Correctional Association, 4321 Hartwick Road, Suite L–208, College Park, MD 20740.

The first title covers personnel and institutions for U.S. states, territories, federal government, and Canada. Includes parole and probation agencies. The second includes more detailed information on over three thousand facilities in the United States.

## PROBATION AND PAROLE

*Directory of United States Probation Officers*. Probation Division, Administrative Office of the U.S. Courts, Washington, DC 20544.

Names, phone numbers, and addresses of two thousand probation officers arranged by district.

*Probation and Parole Directory: United States and Canada*. American Correctional Association, 4321 Hartwick Road, Suite L–208, College Park, MD 20740.

Both organizational and personnel information on over six thousand departments, boards, and courts.

## LAW

*Law and Legal Information Directory*. Gale Research Company, Book Tower, Detroit, MI 48226.

A comprehensive directory to organizations, courts, regulatory agencies, law schools, legal education, scholarships, grants, awards, and information sources.

*Martindale-Hubbell Law Directory*. Martindale-Hubbell, Inc., Box 1001, Summit, NJ 07901.

Lists most lawyers in the United States, its possessions, Canada, and numerous lawyers and law firms abroad. Includes patent lawyers and those in government service.

## INFORMATION SOURCES, EDUCATION, AND EMPLOYMENT

*Directory of Criminal Justice Information Sources*. National Criminal Justice Reference Service, National Institute of Justice, Justice Department, Box 6000, Rockville, MD 20850.

Lists computerized literature search sources, interlibrary loan sources, reference services, and other resource agencies and organizations.

*Directory of Automated Criminal Justice Information Systems*. Bureau of Justice Statistics, Justice Department, Washington, DC 20531.

Details of computerized information systems in operation in police, courts, and corrections agencies at the federal, state, and local levels.

*Criminal Justice Educational Opportunities*. Criminal Justice Center, Sam Houston State University, Huntsville, TX 77341.

State-by-state description of programs available in institutions of higher education. Programs described range from certificates to doctoral degrees.

*Directory of Law-Related Education Projects*. Special Committee on Youth Education for Citizenship, American Bar Association, 1155 E. 60th Street, Chicago, IL 60637.

Geographical arrangement of three hundred-plus law-related education programs in the United States and Canada for teachers and curriculum developers.

*National Employment Listing Service for the Criminal Justice System and Social Services*. Criminal Justice Center, Sam Houston State University, Huntsville, TX 77341.

Lists not only law enforcement openings but also those in correctional agencies, community agencies, and educational programs.

## SERVICES

*National Directory of Children and Youth Services*. CPR Directory Services Company, 1301 20th Street, NW, Washington, DC 20036.

Included here because it covers juvenile court and youth advocacy services and runaway and abuse centers.

*National Ex-Offender Assistance Directory*. P.O. Box 81826, Lincoln, NE 68501.

Intended to link people with problems to existing resources. Under each state and its cities appear names of those agencies, organizations, or persons who offer direct or referral services to ex-offenders.

*The National Prison Directory: A Prison Reform Organizational and Resource Directory with a Special Section on Public Library Service to Prisoners*. Urban Information Interpreters, P.O. Box AH, College Park, MD 20740.

Look at the subtitle for the clue to the thrust of this directory. It provides an overview of the "composition and character of the prison reform movement" in the United States by noting groups active in prison issues.

# Appendix C

# Selected Major National Commission Reports

National commission reports offer insights into the social, political, and economic tenor of the times. They present an overview of a national situation and make specific recommendations. Thus, commission reports provide important information and marvelous background reading for the criminal justice researcher.

Important as these reports are, their publication patterns tend to be confusing with interim reports, subreports, field studies, summary reports, and final reports. Access is often equally as convoluted, since listings in bibliographies and catalogs are not always consistent. Therefore, we are including both the SuDocs call numbers and the popular names of the commissions with the hope that such information will simplify the finding process. Popular names are usually derived from the name of the person chairing the group.

You will find this title helpful in identifying commission reports:

Bernier, Bernard A., and Karen A. Wood. *Popular Names of U.S. Government Reports*. Washington, DC: Library of Congress, 1984.

**1931 Wickersham Commission.**

U.S. National Commission on Law Observance and Enforcement. *Reports*. 14 vols. Washington, DC: U.S. Government Printing Office, 1931. Reprint. Montclair, NJ: Patterson Smith, 1968. (Y3:N21/7:5/#)

Valuable primary and secondary material on the social history of the United States. The fourteen reports are on prohibition; enforcement of prohibition laws; criminal statistics; prosecution; deportation laws; child offenders; federal courts; criminal procedure; penal institutions, probation, and parole; crime and foreign born; lawlessness in law enforcement; cost of crime; causes of crime; and police. Final volume is *The Mooney Billings Report* (on unfairness in prosecution), which was submitted to the commission but not released by it. Commission chaired by George Woodward Wickersham.

**1967 Katzenbach Report**.

U.S. President's Commission on Law Enforcement and Administration of Justice. *Challenge of Crime in a Free Society*. Washington, DC: U.S. Government Printing Office, 1967. (PR 36.8:L41/#)

Indexed report surveying crime and its causes and prevention in the United States. Includes statistics. Chapter headings are: "Crime in America," "Juvenile Delinquency and Youth Crime," "Police Courts," "Corrections," "Organized Crime," "Narcotics and Drug Abuse," "Drunkenness Offenses," "Control of Firearms," "Science and Technology," "Research-Instrument for Reform," and "National Strategy." Chaired by Nicholas DeBelleville Katzenbach.

Published Task Force Reports, which include statistics and references, are available: *The Police, The Courts, Corrections, Juvenile Delinquency and Youth Crime, Organized Crime, Science and Technology, Assessment of Crime, Narcotics and Drugs*, and *Drunkenness*.

Field surveys supporting the commission's findings are: *Report on a Pilot Study in the District of Columbia on Victimization and Attitudes Toward Law Enforcement, Criminal Victimization in the U.S., Studies in Crime and Law Enforcement in the Major Metropolitan Areas, Police in the Community*, and *National Survey of Police and Community Relations*.

**1968 Kerner Commission**.

U.S. National Advisory Commission on Civil Disorders. *Report*. Washington, DC: U.S. Government Printing Office, 1968. (PR 36.8:C49/#)

Covers causes, events, and aftermaths of the civil disorders of 1963 to 1967. Recommendation for improving social conditions which foment riots. City-by-city discussion of disorders. Discusses administration of justice under emergency conditions. Full indexing. Useful statistics. Commission chaired by Otto Kerner.

**1969 Eisenhower Reports**.

U.S. National Commission on the Causes and Prevention of Violence. *To Establish Justice, to Insure Domestic Tranquility*. Washington, DC: U.S. Government Printing Office, 1969. (PR 36.8:V81/#)

This commission emphasized the historical and sociological aspects in carrying out its mission to determine the causes of violence in the United States and to find methods of prevention. Commission chaired by Milton Stover Eisenhower.

Its thirteen-volume *NCCPV Staff Study Series* includes *Task Force Reports* and *Special Investigative Reports*:

vols. 1, 2 *Violence in America: Historical and Comparative Perspectives* (Graham Report)
vol. 3 *Politics of Protest* (Skolnick Report)
vol. 4 *Rights in Concord*

vol. 5 *Shoot-out in Cleveland: Black Militants and the Police*
vol. 6 *Shut It Down: College in Crisis, San Francisco State*
vol. 7 *Firearms and Violence in American Life*
vol. 8 *Assassination and Political Violence*
vol. 9 *Mass Media and Violence*
vol. 9a *Hearings*
vol. 10 *Law and Order Reconsidered*
vols. 11, 12, 13 *Crimes of Violence*

Volumes 4, 5, and 6 above and the following two titles comprise the *Special Investigative Reports*: (1) *Rights in Conflict: The Violent Confrontation of Demonstrators and Police in the Parks and Streets of Chicago During the Week of the Democratic National Convention of 1968 (Walker Report)*; and (2) *Miami Report; Civil Disturbances in Miami, Fla. During the Week of August 5, 1968.*

**1970 Lockhart Reports.**

U.S. Commission on Obscenity and Pornography. *Report.* Washington, DC: U.S. Government Printing Office, 1970–71. (Y3.0b7:#)

Established in 1967, the commission studied the constitutional and definitional problems relating to obscenity controls, traffic in the distribution of obscene and pornographic materials, the effects of such material (particularly on youth), and their relationship to crime and antisocial behavior. Some findings proved highly controversial. Commission chaired by William B. Lockhart.

Technical reports include: *Preliminary Studies; Legal Analysis; Marketplace, Industry; Marketplace, Empirical Studies; Societal Control Mechanisms; National Survey; Erotica and Antisocial Behavior; Erotica and Social Behavior*; and *Consumer and the Community*.

**1970 Scranton Report.**

U.S. President's Commission on Campus Unrest. *Report.* Washington, DC: U.S. Government Printing Office, 1970. (PR37.8:C15/R29)

Special coverage of Kent State and Jackson State Universities is included in this overview of campus unrest during the 1960s. Extensive bibliography. Commission chaired by William W. Scranton.

**1973 Shafer Report.**

U.S. National Commission on Marihuana and Drug Abuse. *Drug Use in America: Problem in Perspective*. Washington, DC: U.S. Government Printing Office, 1973. (Y3:M33/2:#)

Its first report entitled *Marihuana: A Signal of Misunderstanding*, includes a separate appendix volume.

The second and final report examines the roots of the drug problem and suggests ways of reducing its impact. Four volumes note the *Patterns and Consequences of Drug Use, Social Responses to Drug Use, The Legal System and Drug Control*, and *Treatment and Rehabilitation*. Commission chaired by Raymond Philip Shafer.

**1973 Peterson Report.**

U.S. National Advisory Commission on Criminal Justice Standards and Goals. *Reports*. Washington, DC: U.S. Government Printing Office, 1973. (Y3 C86:2C#)

Regarded as the successor of the 1967 President's Commission on Law Enforcement and Administration of Justice, this commission prepared recommendations for crime reduction and prevention on the state and local level. Commission chaired by Russell W. Peterson.

An overview of commission work is given in *A National Strategy to Reduce Crime*. Standards and goals were recommended for these areas: *Community Crime Prevention*, *Corrections*, *Courts*, *Criminal Justice System*, *Police*, and *Juvenile Justice*.

Other reports include:

*Executive Summary: Reports of the National Advisory Commission on Criminal Justice Standards and Goals*, 1974.

*Proceedings of the National Conference on Criminal Justice, Washington, DC*, 1973, 1976.

*A Call for Citizen Action: Crime Prevention and the Citizen*, 1974.

**1975**

U.S. National Advisory Committee on Criminal Justice Standards and Goals. *Reports*. Washington, DC: U.S. Government Printing Office, 1976. (Y3.C86:2#)

Continuing the commission's work, the committee published Task Force Reports intended for the policy maker. Committee chaired by Brendan T. Byrne. Reports deal with: *Criminal Justice Research and Development, Disorders and Terrorism, Juvenile Justice and Delinquency Prevention, Organized Crime, Police Chief Executive*, and *Private Security*.

**1976**

U.S. Commission on the Review of the National Policy Toward Gambling. *Gambling in America*. Washington, DC: U.S. Government Printing Office, 1976. (Y3.G14:1/976–2)

The first national commission to deal with the complex legal, economic, political, and sociological aspects of gambling issued two interim reports previous to this final report. Its charge was to examine the laws and customs that govern gambling and develop uniform guidelines for all levels of government in developing statutory and administrative policies. Report accompanied by three appendices: (1) Staff and Consultant Papers, Model Statistics, Bibliography, Correspondence; (2) Survey of American Gambling Attitudes and Behavior; and (3) Summary of Commission Hearings. Commission chaired by Charles H. Morin.

**1984**

United States Attorney General's Task Force on Family Violence. *Final Report*. Washington, DC: U.S. Government Printing Office, 1984. (J1.2:F21/2)

The Task Force identifies various aspects of family violence, a complex social problem, then lists and discusses recommendations for ameliorative action. Commission chaired by Chief William L. Hart.

# Author-Title Index

# Subject Index

**About the Authors**

MARILYN LUTZKER is Deputy Chief Librarian and Head of Reader Services, as well as Associate Professor at John Jay College of Criminal Justice in New York City. She has contributed chapters to *Teaching the Teachers: On the Job Evaluation for Bibliographic Instruction*, and to the Association of College and Research Libraries proceedings *Options for the Eighties* and *Academic Libraries: Myths and Realities*. Her articles have appeared in *The Bookmark* and *Reference Services Review*.

ELEANOR FERRALL is Reference Librarian and Subject Specialist for Criminal Justice and Public Affairs at Arizona State University. She edited a section of *Arizona Blue Book 1971–72* and the *Arizona Government Publications KWOC Index* (1973–78). She compiled *Fighting Fiscal Containment with Municipal Fees: A Selected Bibliography* and has contributed to *Municipal Government Reference Sources, Research in Education, ACJS Today, Serials Review, Serials Librarian*, and *Women in Forestry*. She reviews books for *American Reference Books Annual* and *Books of the Southwest*.

www.ingramcontent.com/pod-product-compliance
Lightning Source LLC
Chambersburg PA
CBHW051254200926
51612CB00001B/41
*9780313244902*